MAKING THE LINK

Helping Children Link School Habits With the World of Work

Grades 2-5

Lisa King, Ed.S., LPC.

Layout and design by Tonya Daugherty

Edited by Sandy Ragona, MSEd.
and Susan Bowman, Ed.S.

ISBN—1-889636-73-8

Library of Congress Control Number:
2004114202

10 9 8 7 6 5 4 3 2
Printed in the United States

PO Box 115 • Chapin, SC 29036
(800) 209-9774 • (803) 345-1070 • Fax (803) 345-0888
yl@sc.rr.com • www.youthlight.com

Dedication

I would like to dedicate this book to the creative efforts of the women in my family and to all of the counselors who inspire children, parents and, of course, each other.

Acknowledgements

The author would like to acknowledge the contributions of the following people without their help this book would not have been possible.

Thanks to my family: my mother, Joan King, and my sister, Traci King, who contributed their creative genius in creating the poems in this book. They are my cheerleaders and supporters through life. My father, Stephen King, for his pride and confidence in me.

To my friends who are like family… you know who you are. Thank you for believing in me and celebrating life with me.

My team of colleagues who helped me edit this text and also contributed valuable ideas: Dawn Haskett, Lori Armburster, Lori Kotarba, Lundy Semple, Callie Bizner, and Judith Carter.

The Cobb County Counselors who represent the upper echelon of professionals and who participate in the sharing of ideas throughout the years.

Bob Bowman who has walked me through this process with encouragement and advice.

To the students who have touched my life and encouraged me to persevere personally and professionally.

To Susan Bowman and Tonya Daugherty who helped clean up the finished product and worked hard to design and edit this book.

About the Author

Lisa King is an elementary school counselor at Blackwell Elementary School in Marietta, Georgia. She earned a Bachelors of Arts from Tufts University and M.Ed. and Ed.S. degrees from Georgia State in School Counseling. Lisa is a Licensed Professional Counselor and a Nationally Certified School Counselor. In 2003, she was selected as the Cobb County elementary counselor of the year. She resides in Atlanta, Georgia.

Table of Contents

Table of Contents

responsibility
R

Chapter 9: Setting up an Innovative Career Day ..209

MAKING THE LINK:
HELPING STUDENTS LINK ACADEMIC SKILLS TO THE WORLD OF WORK

Recently, I was part of a committee that worked to align local county curriculum to the national standards of the American School Counseling Association. As an elementary counselor, this provided me an opportunity to witness an evolution in the professional development of school counseling. The time has come that local systems across the country are working towards becoming more congruent. In 2003, when our local curriculum in Cobb County, Georgia was structured with the national model, I attempted to gather child-friendly lessons that aligned with the three domains of personal/social, academic, and career. It soon became clear that there is a huge lack of elementary counseling resources, resources in the academic and career domains. I came to realize that the lessons I used were typically homemade lessons and lessons that I creatively modified to fit these domains. This workbook was born out of the idea that counselors needed easy-to-use lessons that directly link academic and career standards to the American School Counselors Association's national model.

The skills addressed within this book include: Responsibility, Career Awareness, Goal Setting, Time Management, Listening Skills, Testing Skills, Learning Styles, and Learning from Mistakes. In an elementary setting these skills are the important competencies to emphasize within the career domain. Not only does ASCA define these as important to include as part of a counseling curriculum, but also these are applicable life lessons that will help students in their academic succes. Creating this book has been exciting because the need for creative, child-friendly lessons in the career academic domains are so lucrative. I hope these lessons are helpful to counselors who are looking to add to their developmental program.

HOW TO USE THE BOOK

Although local systems are making a move to align standards with the national model, each counselor will continue to teach the required curriculum in a different way that he/she feels comfortable. This program was designed to provide the reader with flexibility within the framework. Counselors or educators can use this book in classroom guidance lessons (or small group counseling) in many different ways, to suit their own needs. Annual overviews are provided to help keep track of what strategies work best.

WHAT IS INCLUDED IN EACH CHAPTER:

Parent letter—In each chapter, there is a letter informing the parents of concepts and skills learned in our upcoming guidance lesson. Each letter encourages parents to have a family discussion about how each academic skill links to the world of work.

Pre-Post Student Survey—In each chapter, there is a survey to assess student skill acquisition and perceptions regarding the specific skill. This can help counselors provide data for the accountability that accompanies our job.

Story Connections—There is a story about the specific academic skills covered in that chapter. At the end of each story are questions for review and ideas for extension activities.

Word Searches—These are great reproducibles to reinforce your lesson on that chapter's skill, or to use in centers.

Poems—In each chapter there is a poem and different ways to use the poems. You can hang it in the classroom for the weeks surrounding this lesson. Another idea is that each week a student fills out a job application to be the poet or announcer and if they are selected they have the opportunity to read or recite this poem on the announcements or newscast for the school. Also, the poem can serve as a model for the kids to write their own poem about the chapter topic.

Activities and Reproducible Lessons—For each chapter, there will be reproducible worksheets and lesson plans to explain each activity.

Role Play Cards—These cards are easy to use, copy and laminate. The cards describe different situations that students can act out to practice the positive ways to implement the skills such as responsibility, listening skills, etc.

Office Groups—In order to keep the language of your lessons in terms of careers and the world of work, this program uses small groupings called office groups. It is recommended to split the class into small groups of about 3-6 students in each group. If you choose to have the office groups remain as a cohesive group for a certain number of lessons, you can have the groups create their own group name. Also, icebreaker activities can be done in these groups. In many lessons within this book, office groups are referred to and denote any small group of 3-6 students. These office groups serve many purposes. It's important to train the kids to remember who is in their office groups as a time saver for subsequent lessons. Office groups are an important part of this program not only because working in groups is part of the national standards in the ASCA model, but additionally, it brings the language of careers to the classroom. Office groupings can be used for: Small group discussion, Centers, Game Playing, Cooperative group activities. (see page 13 for visual organizer).

* Please note that with younger children or in certain activities with the older children, you can use "office partners" or dyads. Using the language of "office groups" or "office partners" will help the students make a connection that the classroom is essentially their office.

UNIQUE TOOLS IN THIS BOOK

How to Set up Career Day: A unique section in this book is chapter 9 where there are many ideas for setting up a unique and efficiently organized career day in an elementary school. Additionally there are reproducible letters and handouts that will help with ideas surrounding career day.

Make a Link Game and Question Cards: The two-page spread on pages 238-239 is the Making a Link game. The directions to play the game are on page 236. There are question cards for each chapter category.

Teacher name ______________________

OFFICE GROUPS

For lessons of linking school success to the success skills, discuss with your class the need to be a professional student. Professionals work in offices. For many activities in the next few lessons we will be working in office groups. List the students in each "office group" below. This will be a good reminder in case the students forget what group they are in.

Office Group 1

____
____
____
____
____
____
____
____

Office Group 2

____
____
____
____
____
____
____
____

Office Group 3

____
____
____
____
____
____
____
____

Office Group 4

____
____
____
____
____
____
____
____

Office Group 5

____
____
____
____
____
____
____
____

Office Group 6

____
____
____
____
____
____
____
____

** Please note that with younger children or in certain activities with the older children, you can use "office partners" or dyads. Using the language of "office groups" or "office partners" will help the students make a connection that the classroom is essentially their office.*

Grade Level ____________________________

TEACHER NEEDS ASSESSMENT FOR GUIDANCE TOPICS

WHAT DO YOU WANT ME TO TEACH IN CLASSROOM GUIDANCE?

This year, some of my guidance lessons will teach students how to be "Professional Students." These lessons reinforce skills that you are already teaching in your classrooms. Below is a list of eight topics within the curriculum I will be using called *Making the Link: A program linking academic skills with the world of work.* Through this program, I hope to remind students that they should be treating their job as a student seriously. I am interested in knowing specifically which skills you would like for me to address in my guidance lessons.

Please number the topics 1-8 in the order in which you find these topics a priority (1 being most important to cover, 8 being less of a priority). Thank you for your input.

______ **Responsibility**

______ **Career Awareness**

______ **Goal Setting**

______ **Time Management and Punctuality**

______ **Paying Attention and Listening Skills**

______ **Testing Skills**

______ **Learning Styles**

______ **Learning from Mistakes**

Please return to your counselor and let me know any other way I can help improve the school success skills to your "professional students."

HOW TO USE THIS BOOK WITH SMALL GROUPS

Many counselors focus on study skills in small group counseling. The skills covered in *Making the Link* are the skills that students need to excel in the academic arena. This curriculum can be used in small group counseling. Below is a sample of a group outline that can be used. Counselors can be flexible in choosing what lessons to implement in the outline below.

Attendance

	Name of Members	Permission	1	2	3	4	5	6	7	8
1										
2										
3										
4										
5										
6										
7										
8										

Study Skills Small Group Counseling

	Date	Lesson Activity	Materials Needed	Notes
1		Introduction to group: Group rules, Student Questionnaire	questionnaire page 17	Give teacher the questionnaire on page 16
2				
3				
4				
5				
6				
7		Play Making the Link Game	Making the Link Game (in appendix)	
8		questionnaire page 17, Skittle End of Group Game page 18	questionnaire page 17	Give teacher the questionnaire on page 16

Student in the Group ______________________ Today's Date ______________

TEACHER QUESTIONNAIRE

STUDY SKILLS SMALL GROUP COUNSELING

Teacher: Please fill out this questionnaire to help identify the strengths and weaknesses of your student's study skills. You will be given this again at the end of group to measure what skills this student has gained.

For each statement, please rate the student:

	Strongly Agree	Agree	Disagree	Strongly Disagree
1. This student exhibits effective active listening skills.	❑	❑	❑	❑
2. This student takes responsibility for actions.	❑	❑	❑	❑
3. This student is on time to school often.	❑	❑	❑	❑
4. This student turns in homework on time.	❑	❑	❑	❑
5. This student completes class work.	❑	❑	❑	❑
6. This student accepts mistakes as a way to learn.	❑	❑	❑	❑
7. This student displays a positive attitude about learning.	❑	❑	❑	❑
8. This student seems to have an effective way to study for tests.	❑	❑	❑	❑
9. This students knows how to set realistic goals for him/herself.	❑	❑	❑	❑
10. This student's behavior does not get in the way of learning.	❑	❑	❑	❑
11. This student can recognize the ways that they learn best.	❑	❑	❑	❑
12. This student's desk is organized.	❑	❑	❑	❑

Name ______________________________ Today's Date ____________

STUDENT QUESTIONNAIRE

STUDY SKILLS SMALL GROUP COUNSELING

Please fill out this questionnaire to help identify the strengths and weaknesses of your study skills.

For each statement, please rate yourself:

	Always	Often	Sometimes	Never
1. I show good listening skills.	❑	❑	❑	❑
2. I take responsibility for my actions.	❑	❑	❑	❑
3. I am on time to school.	❑	❑	❑	❑
4. I turn in homework on time.	❑	❑	❑	❑
5. I complete class work.	❑	❑	❑	❑
6. I accept mistakes as a way to learn.	❑	❑	❑	❑
7. I show a positive attitude about learning.	❑	❑	❑	❑
8. I know good ways to study for tests.	❑	❑	❑	❑
9. I know how to set realistic goals for myself.	❑	❑	❑	❑
10. My behavior gets in the way of learning.	❑	❑	❑	❑
11. I know the ways that I learn best.	❑	❑	❑	❑
12. My desk is organized.	❑	❑	❑	❑

THE SKITTLE END OF GROUP GAME

Directions: Color each circle one of the following colors: green, purple, red, yellow, orange. One color will be used twice. Pick a Skittle and answer the question(s) with the same color before eating the Skittle.

For every (S) say one thing that you liked about group.

For every (S) say one thing that has changed in your work habits this year.

For every (S) say something that you still need to improve on.

For every (S) say a goal that you have for the next year.

For every (S) say a responsibility that you have at school or at home.

For every (S) say something that you would change about this group.

Sample of Overview for the

ACADEMIC/CAREER GUIDANCE LESSONS

Each counselor will choose to use this book in different ways. Some counselors spend six weeks on academic and career guidance lessons and some only spend four lessons a year on academic skills depending on how often the counselor goes into the classroom. Below is a sample outline to use to organize lessons in grades 2-5. Counselors can complete this outline with the lessons they have implemented.

	2nd grade	3rd grade	4th grade	5th grade
Punctuality				
Goal Setting				
Responsibility				
Learning from Mistakes				
Testing Skills				
Learning Styles				
Paying Attention and Listening Skills				
Career Awareness				
Career Day				

Congratulations to

______________________________!

You have successfully learned about making the link between your schoolwork and how it will help you in all you do in your life, and the world of work.

Signed ______________________________

CROSSWALK OF INDICATORS

WITHIN ASCA'S NATIONAL MODEL COVERED IN THIS PROGRAM

	Responsibility	Career Awareness	Goal Setting	Time Management	Paying Attention	Testing Skills	Learning Styles	Learn From Mistakes
A:A1.4 Accept mistakes as essential to the learning process	✓	✓	☐	✓	✓	✓	✓	✓
A:A2.3 Use communication skills to know when and how to ask for help when needed	☐	☐	☐	☐	✓	☐	☐	✓
A:A1.5 Identify attitudes and behaviors which lead to successful learning	✓	☐	☐	✓	☐	✓	☐	☐
A:A2.2 Demonstrate how effort and persistence positively affect learning	☐	✓	☐	☐	☐	✓	☐	✓
A:A2.4 Apply knowledge and learning styles to positively influence school performance	✓	✓	☐	✓	✓	✓	☐	✓
A:A2.1 Apply time management and task management skills	✓	✓	☐	✓	☐	✓	☐	☐
A:A3.1 Take responsibility for their actions	✓	☐	☐	☐	☐	☐	✓	✓
A:A3.4 Demonstrate dependability, productivity and initiative	☐	✓	☐	☐	✓	☐	☐	☐
A:B1.3 Apply the study skills necessary for academic success at each level	☐	☐	✓	☐	☐	☐	☐	✓
A:B2.6 Understand the relationship between classroom performance and success in school	☐	☐	☐	☐	☐	✓	☐	✓
C:A1.7 Understand the importance of planning	☐	☐	☐	☐	☐	✓	✓	☐
C:C2.3 Learn to work cooperatively with others as a team member	✓	☐	☐	✓	☐	☐	☐	✓
C:A2.8 Understand the importance of responsibility, dependability, punctuality, integrity and effort in the workplace	✓	✓	☐	☐	☐	☐	☐	☐
C:A2.9 Utilize time and task management skills	✓	✓	☐	✓	✓	✓	✓	☐
PS:A1.8 Understand the need for self-control and how to practice it	☐	☐	☐	☐	☐	☐	☐	☐
PS:A2.6 Use effective communication skills	✓	✓	☐	✓	☐	✓	☐	☐
PS:A2.7 Know that communication involves speaking, listening and nonverbal behavior	☐	☐	☐	☐	✓	☐	☐	☐

Chapter 1

TIME MANAGEMENT AND PUNCTUALITY

Students are often late to school, late on assignments, and often unaware of the importance of punctuality. In this chapter, students can learn about the link between being on time and school/work success. Additionally, staying organized is an important component of being successful. Within this chapter there are many interactive and easy to implement activities that students will learn from and enjoy.

Chapter 1

Indicators from ASCA National Model that are addressed in this chapter (see crosswalk pg 21):

A:A1.5 ....Identify Attitudes and behaviors which lead to successful learning

A:A2.1 ....Apply time management and task management skills.

A:A3.4 ....Demonstrate dependability, productivity and initiative.

C:C2.3 ....Learn to work cooperatively with others as a team member

C:A2.9 ....Utilize time and task management skills

C:A1.10 ..Balance between work and leisure time

Chapter Contents

PRE-POST SURVEY

FOR SKILLS ON TIME MANAGEMENT

Overview: To assess student perception on time management. This pre-post survey can be used in classroom guidance or for a small group for students who are chronically tardy.

ASCA Indicator:
A:A1.5: Identify attitudes and behaviors which lead to successful learning.

Materials Needed:
Time Management Survey

Procedures:

1. Distribute Time Management Survey before the lesson(s) you intend to do on time management.
2. Compile the results to give you an idea of how the group/class feels about time management.
3. Repeat the survey at the end of the lesson(s) to assess what the students have improved on and how perceptions have changed.

Student Survey on Time Management

	Strongly Agree	Agree	Disagree	Strongly Disagree
I am on time for school.	❑	❑	❑	❑
I turn in homework on time.	❑	❑	❑	❑
I think that being on time is important.	❑	❑	❑	❑
I need to improve my time management skills.	❑	❑	❑	❑
Being organized helps me manage my time wisely.	❑	❑	❑	❑
I notice how others feel when I am late.	❑	❑	❑	❑

You may delay, but time will not.

— Benjamin Franklin

Date:

Dear Parent/Guardian,

As adults, it often seems like we don't have enough time to fit everything into a day. As your child is getting older, their responsibilities grow and they may begin to feel the stress of having too much to do. Teaching time management skills at a young age can help to prepare children to plan their time wisely. In your child's guidance lesson/group, we are discussing time management skills and punctuality. We will be discussing how to balance responsibilities and still have time for leisure activities. We will also discuss the importance of being on time to school and on time handing in assignments. These lessons will tie into the need for your child to treat school like a job. On any job, completing task in a timely manner is an important trait. This would be a great time for your family to discuss how to organize time in the after school hours. Thank you for helping your child understand the link between important life skills and school success.

Sincerely,

School Counselor

Activity 1.1

POETRY LINK

I'M ALWAYS LATE

Overview: Students will understand the importance of being on time and the consequences of being late. Through this activity students will explore the importance of being on time in different aspects of life.

ASCA Indicator:

A:A2.1 Apply time management and task management skills

Materials Needed:

Poem page 27

Procedures:

1. Tell class that this is a lesson about punctuality and being on time.
2. Read poem to class.
3. Reiterate how professionals need to use time wisely. Professional counselors need to do this, as do professional teachers, and professional students.
4. Split the class into office groups (see explanation of office groups on page 12).
5. Read poem again. Tell class that this is a poem about being late and now they will have a chance to write their own poem, or rap or even do a skit, or even just give a short story about an incident with the subject they are given.
6. Give each group a punctuality subject card with one of these situations: Late for work, late for school, late turning in an assignment, late for soccer practice, late for an airplane, late for meeting a friend for a movie. (see Activity 1.1 page 28)
7. Remind the groups that they have a time limit.
8. Each group has a turn in presenting their poem or rap song, etc. to the class.
9. Discuss the following questions:
   - How do time limits make you feel?
   - What were some things that made this activity difficult?
   - Why is being on time important?
10. Display poem (page 27) and/or their poems in the classroom to remind students of the lesson about being on time.

Variations:

- In the lesson preceding this, have students fill out a job application (see page 207) if they want to be a "poet." Before the lesson that this poem will be presented, have the selected poet receive a copy of this poem so they can memorize or prepare to perform this poem.
- In center-based guidance this poem can be an activity. Post the poem on page 27 for the students to see as a model. Have the students write poems about or the importance of being on time.

I'M ALWAYS LATE!

BY TRACI KING

Oh no, Oh gosh, Good grief, Oy vey
my alarm did not go off today.

No time to shower or make the bed
Or deal with the mop atop my head.

The dog needs food, oh what a fuss.
If I don't leave now, I'll miss the bus.

Why must this be? I'm always late.
Why is it I procrastinate?

I need a calendar, a PDA
Then perhaps I wouldn't be this way.

If I schedule, to finish my tasks.
I may even have time to sit and relax.

I hope one day that I will see
That rushing only stresses me.

Worksheet 1.1

PUNCTUALITY SUBJECT CARDS

Your office group will create a poem, rap, song, skit or explanation about:

Why is it important for an adult to be on time for work?

Your office group will create a poem, rap, song, skit or explanation about:

Why is it important for students to be on time for school?

Your office group will create a poem, rap, song, skit or explanation about:

Why is it important for students to turn in assignments on time?

Your office group will create a poem, rap, song, skit or explanation about:

Why is it important for kids to be on time for their soccer game?

Your office group will create a poem, rap, song, skit or explanation about:

Why is it important for people to be on time for an airplane flight?

Your office group will create a poem, rap, song, skit or explanation about:

Why is it important to be on time to meet a friend at the movies?

Activity 1.2

STORY CONNECTION
TARDY MARTY

Overview: Through reading a short story and answering questions, students will understand consequences of tardiness.

ASCA Indicator:
C.C2.3 Students will learn to work cooperatively with others as a team member.

A:A3.4 Student will learn to demonstrate dependability, productivity and initiative.

Materials Needed:
Copies of story on pages 30-32 including Tardy Marty Questions.

Procedures:

1. Ask if anyone in the class knows the definition of the word **TARDY**. Discuss the definition.
2. Read story aloud to the class. Hand out copies if you'd like students to read silently while you read aloud.
3. After they have heard the story, divide the class into office groups (see explanation of office groups on page 12).
4. Assign one person in the group to be question reader and one person to be a secretary.
5. The Question Reader reads the questions to the office group.
6. The Secretary writes down the answer that the group discusses.
7. The group then discusses an optional story ending that they come up with for the last question. The Secretary will write the new story ending. (Option: these can be displayed on a bulletin board).
8. At the designated time, the class gets back together as a whole group and a group member can present one question that they discussed.

Activity 1.2

TARDY MARTY
STORY CONNECTION

It wasn't unusual for Martin to be late. Every year since kindergarten he was tardy at least a few times each week, so by the time he was in Ms. Lavender's class in the third grade he had a reputation. And it doesn't take a rocket scientist to realize that his nickname made sense. Marty was tardy all the time… he really was Tardy Marty.

One day in the beginning of third grade, Ms. Lavender pulled him out in the hallway to talk to him "Martin, tell me why you were late."

"I don't know" he responded, "Guess I forgot to set my clock."

The next week, when Ms. Lavender was taking attendance, she asked "Is Martin absent today?"

"No… Marty's Tardy!" Mia yelled out. Mrs. Lavender didn't catch on quite yet that this was a habit. When he got to the class Ms. Lavender took him out in the hall again and asked, "Why are you late today? "

"Uh" he answered, "the honest answer is…" And he wanted to be honest with Ms. Lavender. She was the best teacher he'd ever had. "I was starving and needed a great big breakfast… don't you ever feel like you just have to satisfy that extra hungry feeling with an extra big breakfast?"

Mrs. Lavender grimaced.

The next time Marty was tardy, Ms. Lavender had an idea. This time, she didn't ask him why he was late.

When recess time came, Martin was always the first one to run to the door and today was no different. But at the normal recess time… Martin was on his way out the door at exactly ten–thirty. But Ms. Lavender didn't budge and kept on teaching about map skills.

Five minutes later, Martin was thinking, "Hey, we're missing our outside time and we've earned 3 extra minutes for the compliment we got from Ms. Thomason the music teacher."

Martin was good at math and he was extra good at knowing that they only had 23 minutes between now and lunchtime. He wondered what was wrong with Ms. Lavender…. she never was late to anything. Especially recess time.

Martin raised his hand and said, "Ms. Lavender, I think we are late to go outside."

"Oh my goodness! Oh well. Guess I forgot to set my watch, Martin."

They lined-up and went outside… but only for 16 minutes. Martin wasn't happy.

But, he eventually cheered up, because special snack time came later that day. And since this was Martin's favorite time (other than recess), Martin was counting down the minutes. Especially because today Jade's mom had brought in cupcakes for her birthday. Martin could see them sitting in a box on the counter and the butter cream icing was visible as he sat at his desk.

Ms. Lavender had told the class they would have snack at 1:30 today. But when 1:30 rolled around and Ms. Lavender didn't budge, Martin started to squirm. Ms. Lavender is very strict about silent reading time being SILENT. So Martin just stared at the clock and counted the minutes. All he could concentrate on was the "tick-tock,tick-tock" of the clock.

To make matters worse, Ms. Lavender went over to the cupcake box and started eating a special cupcake in front of all the whole class. Martin couldn't resist, he raised his hand risking breaking the silence and potentially getting a bad note home.

Ms. Lavender smiled, "Yes Martin" She said with her mouth half full.

"Ms. Lavender, isn't it time to pass out the cupcakes to us?"

"Am I late?" Ms. Lavender asked, "Sorry, I was starving."

Martin was so angry. He liked Ms. Lavender a lot but this was not fair and before he knew it he blurted out his thoughts "But that's not fair! You're not paying attention to the time!"

Ms. Lavender with a sneaky smile looked right at Marty, "Don't you ever get so hungry that you have to satisfy that extra hungry feeling?"

Martin started to blurt out something else when he recognized those words. He sat in his seat and closed his eyes. He could feel the whole class looking at him.

And for the rest of that year, Marty wasn't tardy to school anymore.

Worksheet 1.2

TARDY MARTY DISCUSSION QUESTIONS

- What are some of the reasons Martin was late to school?

  ____

  ____

- What are other reasons kids are late for school?

  ____

  ____

- How do teachers feel when students are late?

  ____

  ____

- How could Martin make sure to be at school on time?

  ____

  ____

- What are some reasons teachers want students to come to school on time?

  ____

  ____

- Write a story about the beginning of Martin's fourth grade year. Did he maintain his on time behavior or did he return to his old tardy ways?

  ____

  ____

  ____

  ____

Activity 1.3

WORD SEARCH

BEING ON TIME

Overview: Word puzzles are a great way to supplement a lesson on time management or the activity below can be a lesson unto itself. The purpose of this activity is to understand the effect that time has on us.

ASCA Indicator:
A:A2.1 Apply time management and task management skills

Materials Needed:
Worksheet 1.3 Word Search opposite page, timer

Procedures:

1. Facilitator distributes word search.
2. Tell the students that they will have a time limit to complete the word search. (Approximately 10 minutes)
3. Set the timer.
4. When the time limit is up, tell the students to put their pencils down.
5. Process the activity by telling the class that this lesson truly is about time limits and trying to understand the effect that time limits have on us.
6. Ask the following discussion questions and have students respond.

Discussion Questions:

a. What were the feelings you had when you were told there was a time limit?

b. What were your thoughts or feelings when I said "Time's up!"

c. What are situations kids at school or adults at work have to deal with on time limits?

d. Did anyone "win" today? (Some kids might try to tell you how many they got right… but the answer is "No one won or lost but this was an exercise for you to see if you work quickly or slowly when under a time limit. If you are a slower worker, it's not a bad thing but it does mean you need to allot more time for yourself when you have a deadline.)

e. How do the words in the word search relate to being on time?

Variations:

- After the discussion questions, have the office teams work together for the remainder of the time. Finish the lesson by discussing how teamwork makes jobs easier.
- Use this to start or end a lesson using a book on punctuality.
- Use the word search as a center.

Worksheet 1.3

Name: ______________________________

ATTENDANCE	PUNCTUALITY
BUS	RESPECT
CLOCK	SCHEDULE
CONSEQUENCE	TARDY
DEADLINES	TIME
LATE	WATCH

How many words did you find in the allotted time? ____________________

Q Q S U E A Q U S C Y S J I N
A T T E N D A N C E T R D H E
D P K E B K J R H J I B W C Q
V E M C E U E C E H L Z N T M
D I A N O S S M D T A E E A B
T C P D P L Z Z U R U E O W N
O H E E L F C D L Q T N M J T
X B C O O I P B E R C B V F X
R T J X G K N S U U N E C N K
Y D R A T J N E S O U D Z U Y
K Z K G F O W H S G P Q M Y A
B C N F C E A I M N Y E I B C
N D J G D I Q B Z A F X Q F O
I B Q M F U L C N Q A O Y E X
L A T E M P C T H L N J E H Y

Activity 1.4

1, 2, 3 ACTION ROLE PLAY

PUNCTUALITY

Overview: Students will act out situations where punctuality, time management and tardiness lead to natural consequences.

ASCA Indicator:
A:A2.1 Apply time management and task management skills.

Materials Needed: Punctuality role-play cards on the following page and Worksheet 1.4 on page 38.

Procedures:

1. Introduce the lesson by discussing the meaning of punctuality.
2. Split the class into office groups (see explanation of office group pg 12)
3. Assign one 'Timer' in the class. Assign jobs within each office groups: Actors, Director (use job cards on page 37)
4. Distribute a role-play card to each group. (Copy the role play cards on page 38)
5. Explain to class that we will be in our office groups for only 10 minutes and the skits should be no more than one minute. The Timer should keep track of these time limits.
6. The Director's role is to oversee decision-making and helping to direct the skit. A good director isn't bossy, but is there to oversee and help make decisions.
7. The Actors should practice and then all students in the group should sit with their heads down in order to let the facilitator know the group is ready.
8. To begin the skit the facilitator will say, "1,2,3 Action" similar to a director in Hollywood. Encourage the students to clap when you say action.
9. Practice "1,2,3 Action" (with everyone clapping in unison when "Action" is said.)
10. The Director from the first office group introduces their group and the counselor leads the class in saying "1,2,3 Action" to signal the group to perform. Subsequently, other groups perform.
11. After the skits, the facilitator leads a discussion asking these questions:
    - Why is being on time so important?
    - Who needs to be responsible for being on time?
    - What things can career professionals and professional students do to make sure they are on time?
    - What are some consequences for being late?
    - (Ask the timer) What were your feelings about being responsible for the time?

Activity 1.4

OFFICE GROUP JOB CARDS

TIMER

Thanks for keeping track of the time!

ACTOR

DIRECTOR

You will oversee decision-making & help direct the skit.

ACTOR

ACTOR

ACTOR

Worksheet 1.4

ROLE PLAY CARDS

Small groups of students can practice these role-plays and then perform in front of the class to illustrate the importance of being on time.

A student has overslept and is very concerned with what outfit to wear. The mom/ dad tries to get the student to the bus on time. The student thinks out loud to him/herself about what to do differently to make sure they are on time the next day. *(2 actors)*

Punctuality Role Play Card #1

A doctor is on time for work everyday. A mother and sick child have a conversation in the waiting room wondering whether the doctor is on time. The responsible doctor is there on time and helps the child. *(2-3 actors)*

Punctuality Role Play Card #2

A student comes to school on time but likes to visit other teachers and friends in the building. He/she is late to class and misses a morning work quiz. *(2-4 actors)*

Punctuality Role Play Card #3

A pilot is on his way through the airport and stops to have a bite to eat. The flight attendant at the gate tells him that the plane left without him. *(2-4 actors)*

Punctuality Role Play Card #4

A student pretends to be sick so he or she doesn't have to go to school. The parent gives the child some advice about how attendance to school will help with school success. *(2 actors)*

Punctuality Role Play Card #5

A student has a lot of homework. The students mom or dad explains that before play time, the student needs to do 20 minutes of homework. Then he/she earns 20 minutes of play time and then needs to return to homework until it is done. *(2 actors)*

Punctuality Role Play Card #6

Activity 1.5

HOW DO YOU MANAGE YOUR TIME?

Overview: Students will learn to be aware of how they spend time and discuss ways to balance their schedules and manage their time.

ASCA indicator:
A:A2.1 The student will apply time management and task management skills.

C:A2.9 Utilize time and task management skills

C:A1.10 Balance between work and leisure time

Procedures:

1. Make double sided copies of worksheet 1.5A and 1.5B. (for grades 2-3 only make copies of 1.5A)
2. Distribute double-sided worksheet to students.
3. Explain how adults use daily time planners like these to make sure that we get everything done. As you get older, you will have more things to do: more homework, more after school activities, more desire to talk on the phone for hours, etc. In order to fit it all in, it's important to make time for important responsibilities. This concept is called time management.
4. Put a sample of worksheet 1.5A on an overhead or show them a similar chart on the board.
5. • For 2nd-3rd grades ask them to fill out what they did from after school until dinner or ask them to fill in when they ate dinner and then four other blocks.

   • For 4-5th grade: ask students to fill out the calendar with what they did yesterday or what they plan on doing today in the after school hours.
6. Give five minutes for this activity. When you see that most people are done with this task, explain to the class that on the back (worksheet 1.5B) they will graph how much time they spend on certain tasks. For instance if they watched TV for 30 minutes that day, they will fill in the bar graph up to the number 30. If they did any activity for more than 60 minutes, they will graph to the top of the graph.
7. When students are finished ask one or two to come up and present their graphs.
8. Ask students these discussion questions:
   - What did you learn at how you spend your time?
   - Were you surprised at how much time you spent doing an activity?
   - Do you think making a time planner would help with time management?
   - How would this be helpful for adults in their careers?
   - Who would benefit most from using a daily planner? What professionals do you think use a planner?

Worksheet 1.5A

HOW DO YOU MANAGE YOUR TIME?

Directions:
Think about what you did yesterday, or one day this past week. List the activity that you were doing at that time in each time block.

2:00	______________	7:00	______________
2:30	______________	7:30	______________
3:00	______________	8:00	______________
3:30	______________	8:30	______________
4:00	______________	9:00	______________
4:30	______________	9:30	______________
5:00	______________	10:00	______________
5:30	______________	10:30	______________
6:00	______________	11:00	______________
6:30	______________	11:30	______________

What activity did you spend the most time?

____

____

____

How would making a time management schedule be helpful?

____

____

____

Worksheet 1.5B

HOW DO YOU MANAGE YOUR TIME?

Look at the time management planner on the previous page.
Think about what you were doing at that time in each time block.

Write how much you spent doing the following activities:

Eating:	______________	Playing Outside:	______________
Homework:	______________	Watching TV:	______________
Sports:	______________	Chores:	______________

Color in the bar graph according to how many minutes
you spend after school doing each activity in a typical day.

time in minutes						
more						
60						
50						
40						
30						
20						
10						
activities:	*watch TV*	*do homework*	*sports*	*chores*	*eat*	*play outside*

Chapter 1

Activity 1.6

MAKING LINKS

Overview: The book title, Making the Link, promotes the concept of making the link between academic skills with success in the world of work. In this activity, students will make paper links regarding the specific skill set taught in this chapter.

ASCA Indicators:
A:A1.5 Identify Attitudes and behaviors which lead to successful learning

A:A2.1 Apply time management and task management skills.

Materials: Strips of construction paper cut vertically into 3″ strips, stapler

Procedures:

1. Cut strips of construction paper.
2. At the end of the lesson on time management, assign a student to be the "Detective" of the week (you can deem the title Guidance Detective or Link Detective if you'd prefer).
3. Have a location in the classroom where the strips of paper (or links) will be for the week(s) in-between the lesson.
4. At the end of each day, or at a designated time, the classroom teacher lets the Detective choose a student (or two students) that they have noticed that day who exhibited the concept of punctuality or meeting deadlines with assignments.
5. The chosen students write on the back of the strip of construction paper an explanation of how they exhibited time management or punctual behavior.
6. Stapling the strip of construction paper from end to end, creating a paper circle, makes the first link. To make the link strand, put the second strip of paper through the circle just created and staple the two ends of this strip so that they are now connected.
7. The class can make the link strand and hang it in their classroom or can bring the link to the counselor who might display the link in his/her office area.

Variation:
Have the classes display the chain of link in the hallway.

**** Please Note: This activity can be generalized to each chapter in this book.***

Activity 1.7

SCHOOL-WIDE LINK:
TARDY BUSTERS PROGRAM

Overview: This school-wide program includes information for parents and student incentive components.

ASCA Indicator:
A:A2.1 Apply time management and task management skills.

Materials: Parent letter, golden clock signs, tardy busters sign, class winner sign, a gold alarm clock (gold alarm clocks are available at discount stores)

Procedures:

1. Gather data about tardies at your school for one month.
2. Educate the local school staff about this program.
3. Send parent letter home (Parent Letter 1.7 on page 44)
4. Hang signs 1.7A and 1.7B (pages 45-46) throughout the school to inspire curiosity.
5. The next week make an announcement explaining Tardy Busters saying: "Tardy Busters is finally here! Many of you have been wanting to find out more about Tardy Busters and the Golden Clock. Tardy Busters is a program where we will have a contest to see which class in each grade level can have the least amount of tardies per week. If your class succeeds, then you get the golden clock for that week. The class with the overall best tardies for the month will get a special prize. (Prize can be a lunch with the principal, popcorn party, etc.)
6. Compile data at the end of each week and make announcement deeming the Golden Clock Awards each Friday afternoon for a month. Bring a golden clock and sign 1.7C to each winner.
7. To follow up with results to parents, publish an article in the school newsletter such as the one on page 48.

Variations:
Let your local newspaper know about your program. If the program proves successful, you can extend the program to subsequent months and invite a local television station out to view the success.

Display a chart in the cafeteria with each weekly winners or each class's total numbers of tardies per week.

Activity 1.7

Date:____________________

Dear Parent/Guardian,

One of the important aspects of students' academic success is the amount of time they spend in the classroom. When students are absent or arrive late, they lose important opportunities to learn. Excessive tardies and absences can prevent children from succeeding academically and socially. Valuable instructional time is missed, the teacher's lesson is interrupted and unnecessary disruption is created for students.

Often, tardy students feel a sense of anxiety and frustration as the school day has started and they already feel behind. The tardy student does not always have time to settle in before the school day actually begins. Many important tasks happen at the start of the day including putting away backpacks, getting out folders, homework, and teacher notes and putting them in their proper places, doing morning work, etc. When the bell rings at _______, students should be ready to begin the day.

The personal habit of on-time attendance is one that will help our students succeed in whatever career they choose for their future lives in the world of work. It is not too early to start talking about how punctuality is an important life skill. You can help your child arrive on time to school by having them ride the bus. If a bus is running late, the child is not counted as tardy. If you do choose to drive your child to school, we encourage you to establish a set time to leave your house that ensures on-time arrival.

For the month of ___________ we had __________ students tardy at _______________ Elementary. Next month, we will be starting a program to reduce the school-wide number of tardies. Our program will be called:

There will be weekly competition between classes in each grade level with the winners getting to keep the "Golden Clock" in their classroom for the whole week. There will also be a prize for the class that shows the most improvement.

Thank you for your support,

School Counselor

Sign 1.7A

The Golden Clock Is Coming...

Sign 1.7B

Is
Coming...

Sign 1.7C

_____________________'s Class
is the winner of the
golden clock award
for the week of
____
The Golden Clock Award

Activity 1.7

Sample of Newsletter Article after the Tardy Busters has been implemented

Counselors Corner

We would like to tell you about our Tardy Busters program for this school year. We collected data on the number of tardies for each class in each grade in order to get a baseline for comparison. Our total number of tardies for the month of _________ was ____. After implementing Tardy Busters, the month of _______________ we had ______________ tardies. We saw a definite need for improvement. We have had very positive reactions from students, parents, and teachers. We even had some students asking their parents to schedule doctor and dentist appointments after the start of school. They did not want to be tardy!

We have definitely seen improvement in many of the classes, but there is room for improvement in others. We encourage you to assist your student or students in their efforts to get to school on time. Being in the classroom ready to begin the day when the bell rings makes for a good start to everyone's day.

Congratulations to all who improved their punctuality.
The winners for the month of ___________ are:

Kindergarten: _______________

First Grade: _______________

Second Grade: _______________

Third Grade: _______________

Fourth Grade: _______________

Fifth Grade: _______________

We also want to acknowledge all of those students who made improvement in being at school on time and thank you, parents, for reinforcing the importance of punctuality. Your contribution to your child's school success is essential and appreciated!

Chapter 2

GOAL SETTING

Our daily lives are full of goals we set for ourselves. Some are long-term goals that take years to accomplish and some are short-term goals that involve our daily tasks. Whether large or small, goals take time and planning to accomplish. Goal setting is a concept that students should be exposed to at an early age, so they can understand how to set goals and plan to accomplish the things they want to achieve.

Chapter 2

Indicators from ASCA National Model that are addressed in this chapter (see crosswalk pg 21):

A:A1.5	Identify Attitudes and behaviors which lead to successful learning
A:A2.2	Demonstrate how effort and persistence positively affect learning.
A:A3.1	Take responsibility for their actions
A:A3.4	Demonstrate dependability, productivity and initiative.
C:A1.6	Learn how to set goals.
PS-B1.9	Identify long and short-term goals.
PS-B1.12	Develop an action plan to set and achieve realistic goals.

Chapter Contents

PRE-POST SURVEY
FOR SKILLS ON GOAL SETTING

Overview: To assess student perception on goal setting. This pre-post survey can be used in classroom guidance or for a small group.

ASCA Indicator:
A:A1.5: Identify attitudes and behaviors which lead to successful learning.

Materials Needed:
Goal Setting Survey

Procedures:

1. Distribute Goal Setting Survey before the lesson(s) you intend to do on Goal Setting.
2. Compile the results to give you an ideas of how the group/class feels about time management.
3. Repeat the survey at the end of the lesson(s) to assess what the students have improved on and how perceptions have changed.

Student Survey on Goal Setting

	Strongly Agree	Agree	Disagree	Strongly Disagree
I set goals for myself everyday.	❑	❑	❑	❑
I should meet every goal I set for myself.	❑	❑	❑	❑
Setting goals helps me do well in school.	❑	❑	❑	❑
I can set goals for school and for home.	❑	❑	❑	❑
Adults must set goals for themselves.	❑	❑	❑	❑

Goals are dreams with deadlines

— Diana Scharf Hunt

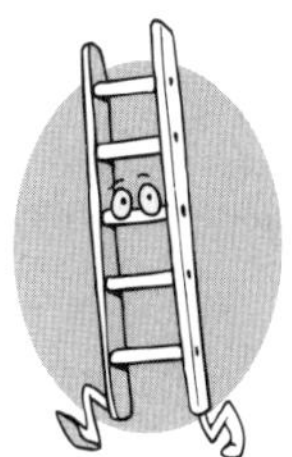

Date:

Dear Parent/Guardian,

We all have goals that we strive to achieve. In fact, our daily lives are full of goals we set for ourselves. Some are long-term goals that take years to accomplish and some are short-term which involve daily tasks. Whether large or small, goals take time and planning to accomplish. Goal Setting is a concept that students should be exposed to at an early age so they can understand how to plan to accomplish things they want to achieve. In our guidance lesson, we will be discussing goal setting. We will be equating goal setting to climbing a ladder. We will do a lot of talking about taking small steps. This would be a great time to discuss goals you have set for yourself so that your child can see how goal setting is an important skill. It is also a great time to ask your child what some goals he/she has for this year. Thank you for helping your child understand the link between life skills and school success.

Sincerely,

School Counselor

Activity 2.1

POEM & STORY CONNECTION

Overview: Students will understand the importance of taking small steps to achieve a goal.

ASCA Indicators:
C.C2.3 Learn to work cooperatively with others as a team member

PS-B1.12 Develop an action plan to set and achieve realistic goals.

Materials: Poem (page 53)

Procedures:

1. Read the poem to the class. (Poem on page 53)
2. After reading the poem aloud, have students work with a partner to discuss the following questions.
    - What are some times that you might need or want to set goals?
    - How can students set goals for class work? What about homework?
3. Read story *Can't jump to the top of the ladder* (page 54)

4. Have students work in pairs and create a poem about a task they would have to work to achieve. An example of a poem title would be *You have to walk before you crawl*. Allow students to come up with their own example. They can raise their hand if they need help. (Option: you can write down these examples on an index card and pass them out if students prefer.)
5. Discuss the following questions:
    - What was the goal that Sara wanted to accomplish?
    - What steps did she need to take to reach her goal?
    - What did Coach Cindy mean about "not being able to jump to the top of the ladder"?
    - What are common goals for peers at school?

REACHING A GOAL

BY TRACI KING

I have a great big task at hand, there's so much to complete
I really want to get this done, not such an easy feat.
It's like a ladder standing tall, that now I have to climb
To finish what I need to do, against the ticks of time.

When looking at so much to do, seems like it won't be fun
But with a brand new attitude, this project will get done.
See, once my goals seems reachable it doesn't seem so bad.
In time I know I'll reach my goal and, oh boy, will I be glad.

If I start to set small goals and examine what's at stake.
My goal to do the task at hand will be a piece of cake!
At the end I'll look back at what seemed to be so tall
I'll look down from the ladder, the goal accomplished after all!

Activity 2.2

CAN'T JUMP TO THE TOP OF THE LADDER

STORY CONNECTION

Sara was very excited to join the gymnastics team when she was in the fourth grade. She saw how her older sister won blue and red ribbons and she couldn't wait to get some of those ribbons for her own bedroom wall. When the day finally arrived for her first gymnastics lesson, she was so excited that it was hard for her not to sprint into the gym. But her mom held her hand as they walked in the door.

Her coach introduced herself and the class began. Coach Cindy started to teach the group of beginners how to do a somersault. They learned how to walk across the balance beam and they learned lots of different names of the tumbling stunts. They did a lot of stretching and had a great day.

The second day of Sara's gymnastics lessons, her coach had them review their somersaults and taught them the correct way to do a cartwheel. Sara raised her hand, "I want to try a front flip instead! I watch my sister all the time so I know I can do it. Can I try?"

"No Sara. For now we have to start at the beginning," said Coach Cindy. Sara pouted. Her eyes welled up and she started to say something else. But instead she bit her lip and followed directions. She did her cartwheels perfectly, but she stayed in a bad mood. That day, when they finished up their lesson, Coach Cindy asked Sara to stay after class.

Her coach pointed to a ladder that was leaning against the gym wall and asked Sara, "You see the ladder? How would you climb up that ladder?" Sara was confused. "What do you mean?" she asked?

Coach Cindy repeated the question and walked closer to the ladder. "How would you climb this ladder?"

Sara answered, “Start right there.” She pointed to the bottom rung.

Her coach smiled, “Right. You can’t jump to the top of the ladder.” It’s the same with any goal you set for yourself. You have to imagine that the goal you want to accomplish is sitting at the top of the ladder. If you want to get to that goal, you have to climb up to it… step by step. I have never seen anyone jump to the top of a tall ladder.” Sara smiled. Cindy continued, “It is the same for doing front flips. You can't just start off doing front flips you have to take small steps to get up to that goal.”

Sara’s eyes started to light up. “So you mean, the first step is to learn how to do a somersault. And the second step” she pointed, “is to learn to do a cartwheel?

“Exactly!” said Cindy. Sara stepped up on the first step of the ladder and looked up. “Wow” she said… “It’s a long way to go. But I know I can do it.”

Cindy smiled and knew the ribbons would one day appear on Sara’s wall.

Activity 2.3

WORD SEARCH
GOAL SETTING

Overview: Students will set a goal as to how many words they thing they can find in a given time. Students will evaluate if they have set realistic goals and will generalize this concept

ASCA Indicator:
PS-B1.12 Develop an action plan to set and achieve realistic goals.

C:A1.6 Learn how to set goals

Materials: Goal Setting Word Search

Procedures:

1. Distribute the word search to the class.
2. Give the class a time limit of how long they will have. (approximately 6 minutes)
3. Before you start the time, have them set a goal of how many words they will find within the time limit and write it in the blank on the bottom.
4. When time is up, have the students write down how many words they actually found.
5. Discussion Questions
    - Would you change your goal next time?
    - Do you like to challenge yourself?
    - How do you challenge yourself in everyday life?

Activity 2.3A

WORD SEARCH
GOAL SETTING

HOW MANY WORDS CAN I FIND?

Name: ____________________________

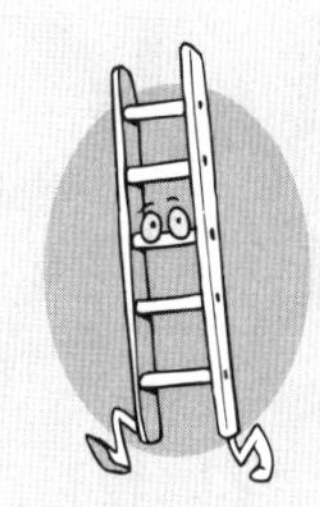

ACCOMPLISH	**GOAL**
IDEA	**LADDER**
LONG-TERM	**PLAN**
REALISTIC	**SHORT-TERM**
STEPS	

1. I set my goal at finding _________ words.
2. I actually found ________ words.
3. I ❑ met, ❑ did not meet, ❑ went beyond my goal.
4. Next time , I would set my goal at _________ words.

H	I	K	Z	P	T	Q	J	P	L	R
A	C	C	O	M	P	L	I	S	H	E
S	Q	I	N	A	R	A	L	S	W	A
H	H	A	S	I	K	O	G	G	M	L
M	L	O	U	P	N	G	N	G	M	I
P	U	T	R	G	E	E	D	V	R	S
H	G	J	T	T	Q	T	Z	U	J	T
F	U	E	C	L	T	F	S	O	R	I
Z	R	V	W	I	D	E	A	W	H	C
M	R	E	D	D	A	L	R	U	Y	Y
G	I	M	K	Z	A	X	T	M	M	G

Activity 2.3B

HOW MANY WORDS CAN I FIND?

Name: ____________________

ACCOMPLISH
IDEA
LONG-TERM
REALISTIC
STEPS
GOAL
LADDER
PLAN
SHORT-TERM

1. I set my goal at finding ________ words.
2. I actually found ________ words.
3. I ❑ met, ❑ did not meet, ❑ went beyond my goal.
4. What did you learn from this exercise?

____

____

R Q F H N B E P D M S
F E I S A U A T R T Z
M B A I L X U E E H A
D H R L P N T P D B L
L N J P I T S O W I A
T J R M R S L Q J D D
B E L O N G T E R M D
U X H C U A J I E E E
I S A C L A O G C L R
V G D A Y E D Z E Q P
J Y W J Q K M P A O S

Activity 2.4

1, 2, 3 ACTION ROLE PLAY

GOAL SETTING

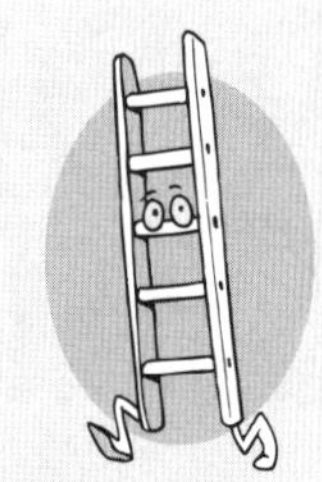

Overview: Students will act out situations where punctuality, time management and tardiness lead to natural consequences.

ASCA Indicator:
PS-B1.12 Develop an action plan to set and achieve realistic goals.

Materials: Role-play cards (pg 60)

Procedures:

1. Introduce the lesson by asking "What is a goal?" Explain a basketball goal, soccer goal, goal to finish a race. A goal is a wish that you take steps to accomplish.
2. Split the class into office groups (see explanation of office group pg 12)
3. Distribute a role-play card to each group. (Copy the role play cards on page 60)
4. Explain to class that we will be in our office groups for a short time and the skits should be no more than one minute.
5. Assign a Director in each group. The director's role is to oversee decision-making and helping to direct the skit. A good director isn't bossy, but is there to oversee and help make decisions if there is an argument.
6. The actors should practice and all students in the group should sit with their heads down when they are ready to let the facilitator know the group is ready.
7. To begin the skit the facilitator explains that to start the skits we will act like Hollywood and we will count to three, clap in unison and say action to begin each skit.
8. Practice "1,2,3 Action."
9. The Director from the first office group introduces their group and the counselor leads the class in saying 1,2,3 Action to signal the group to perform. Subsequently, other groups perform.
10. After the skits, the counselor leads a discussion asking these questions:
    - What are important steps to setting goals?
    - What are important behaviors that make goals easier to reach?
    - In these role-plays, what goals do you think will really get accomplished by these characters?
    - What makes you believe certain people will accomplish goals?

Activity 2.4

ROLE PLAY CARDS

Small groups of students can practice these role-plays and then perform in front of the class to illustrate the importance of being on time.

A team is having a difficult time scoring goals in their soccer games. The coach discusses with the player the steps needed to score a soccer goal.

Goal Setting Role Play Card #1

A runner talks to a group of friends about training for a 5-mile race and what might get in the way of accomplishing this goal. They discuss how you have to improve a little at a time to reach a long-term goal.

Goal Setting Role Play Card #2

A group discusses their science project. They are doing a group project on the solar system and need to divide responsibilities in order to accomplish the goal.

Goal Setting Role Play Card #3

A mechanic has three cars to work on in four hours. He/she discusses with the boss how he/she is going to plan to accomplish this goal.

Goal Setting Role Play Card #4

A group of friends are planning a party for the upcoming weekend. They don't have much time to accomplish the goal. They discuss that they need teamwork to accomplish a goal.

Goal Setting Role Play Card #5

A student wants to be a lawyer when he/she grows up. He /she discusses with his/her parent how this goal will be accomplished.

Goal Setting Role Play Card #6

Activity 2.5

TRASHBALL AND THE LADDER OF SUCCESS

GOAL SETTING

Overview: Through a game and group activity, students will examine the steps necessary to accomplish goals.

ASCA Indicator:
PS-B1.12 Develop an action plan to set and achieve realistic goals.

Materials: A trashcan (or a bucket or tub), 4 balled up pieces of paper (or tennis balls), ladder worksheet (page 63), goal cards (page 62)

Procedures:

1. Have the class split up into office groups.
2. Have the office groups come up with a group name. Review goals setting steps up the ladder. Discuss how having a plan makes things more organized and goals are easier to reach.
3. Invite one person from each team up to the front. Have each student ball up paper and stand across from the trashcan. Tell the students that they are representing their teams and will try to throw 3 baskets. Have them guess how many out of three they will get in the trash. Tell them they can stand wherever they want to. See how many they can get.
4. At the end, review whether the students met their goals. Ask if they did this again, what goal would they set?
5. Discuss how people set a goals for themselves and different desire to set high goals. Did they stand close or far away. If they accomplished their goal the first time did they challenge themselves the second time?
6. Hand out ladders and goals (see pages 62-63). Remind them from last lesson that you can't jump to the top of a ladder. Have each group write the specific skills they would need to accomplish their assigned goal.
7. Have one representative from each group tell about how they would reach that goal.

Activity 2.5

GOAL CARDS

YOUR GOAL:

Make a Peanut Butter And Jelly Sandwich

YOUR GOAL:

Win the spelling bee

YOUR GOAL:

Become the star pitcher on the softball team

YOUR GOAL:

Make a new friend

YOUR GOAL:

Earn enough money to buy a new game

YOUR GOAL:

Make a snowman

Worksheet 2.5

Come up with the steps you would take to achieve your goal. Remember start from the bottom and work your way up.

What is your goal?

A LETTER TO ME, FROM ME:
WHAT WILL MY GOALS BE?

Overview: This activity can be done in class or centers to understand how goals might change over time.

ASCA Indicator:
PS-B1.9 Identify long and short-term goals.

Materials: A letter to me, from me (worksheet 2.6), ideas for goals (poster 2.6)

Procedures:

1. Ask students to think about what they wanted to be when they grow up. Ask them to think whether they would have answered this question differently when they were in kindergarten.
2. Define long-term goals as things you want to do in the far off future (a month or a year). These goals can become possible if there is planning. Short-term goals (goals to accomplish in hours or days) also require planning.
3. Ask if anyone has changed goals in what after school sport/activity they wanted to pursue. Discuss how sometimes long term goals change.
4. Distribute the goal letter (page 65). Tell the class, "You will write letters to yourself from yourself."
5. Put Poster 2.6 on board in front of class to give them ideas of goals that they can write in their letter.
6. Tell students that they can put this letter away in a diary, or under their mattress or in a drawer and look at it next year and see if their goals have changed.
7. Discussion questions:
   - Do you think these goals will change by the end of the year? In two years?
   - What factors might play a role in changing your goals?
   - Who will help you accomplish your goals?

Variation: The counselor can collect the letters and give the letters back to students at a later date or even have students bring a self-addressed stamped envelope to the counselor and the counselor can later send the letter to the student. Remind the students that you will not send their letter if it is incomplete. The counselor can attach the note below with the letter sent.

Hello!

Last year, you wrote yourself a letter about goals you hoped to accomplish. I hope that you are achieving all of your goals. Best Wishes!

Signed,
Your counselor

Worksheet 2.6

A LETTER TO ME, FROM ME:
WHAT WILL MY GOALS BE?

Date _______________

Dear ________________________,
(write your full name here)

I am ___ years old and in the ____ grade. Below I have listed goals I have for myself at home, at school, and in my personal life.

This year at school my goal is ____________________________________

____.

At home, my goal is ____

____.

Another goal I have is ____

____.

A long-term goal is something I want to accomplish in the far off future. My long-term goal is ____________________________________

____.

I think I can accomplish this goal by the time I am ____ years old. In order to accomplish this goal I will need to do the following things: __________

____

____

____

____

Signed,

____

Chapter 2

Poster 2.6

IDEAS FOR GOALS

- Do better in math or reading
- Read more books
- Play an instrument
- Have better handwriting
- Have more friends
- Be in chorus
- Raise your hand in class
- Be on a sports team
- Make Fun Friday more often
- Show self-control on the bus
- Be on student council
- Getting along with brothers/sisters
- Cleaning room without having to be asked

Activity 2.7

ROLL A GOAL

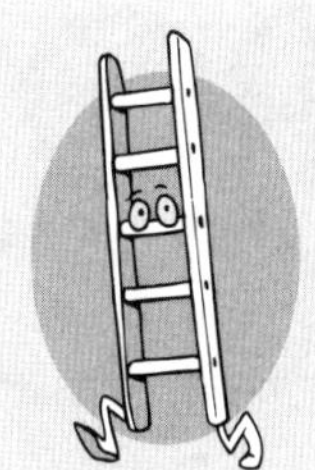

Overview:

ASCA Indicator:

Materials:

Procedures:

1. Make 2 copies of this paper die template. Cut out each template and glue tabs to create dice.

2. On one of the templates write one of the following words on each side of the die so that all sides have a word on them:

   Short Term

   Long Term

   Free Turn

3. On one of the templates write one of the following words on each side of the die so that all sides have a word on them:

   School

   Career

   Friends

   Home

   Sports

   Family

4. In office groups (see page 12 for explanation), each player has a turn to roll both dice at once and depending on what they roll, they tell a long or short term goal they have about a certain aspect of their life.

Worksheet 2.7

ROLL A GOAL

glue

glue

glue

glue

glue

glue

glue

Chapter 3

RESPONSIBILITY

The ability to admit wrongdoings and take responsibility for our behavior is an important thing for children to learn at a young age. The characteristic of being responsible is important for students at home and at school. Children of all ages need to have responsibility and understand why it is important to follow through with what is expected of us. In this chapter there are many exercises to help students understand the importance of taking responsibility for themselves.

responsibility

R

Chapter 3

Indicators from ASCA National Model that are addressed in this chapter (see crosswalk pg 21):

A:A1.5 ......Identify attitudes and behaviors, which lead to successful learning

A:A3.1 ....Take responsibility for their actions

A:A3.4 ....Demonstrate dependability, productivity and initiative.

C:A2.8......Understand the importance of responsibility, dependability, punctuality, integrity and effort in the workplace

C.C2.3......Learn to work cooperatively with others as a team member

Chapter Contents

PRE-POST SURVEY

RESPONSIBILITY

Overview:

ASCA Indicator:
A:A1.5: Identify attitudes and behaviors which lead to successful learning.

Materials Needed:
Responsibility Survey

Procedures:

1. Distribute Responsibility Survey before the lesson(s) you intend to do on Responsibility.
2. Compile the results to give you an idea of how the group/class feels about Responsibility.
3. Repeat the survey at the end of the lesson(s) to assess what the students have improved on and how perceptions have changed.

Student Survey on Responsibility

	Strongly Agree	Agree	Disagree	Strongly Disagree
I take responsibility for my actions at home.	❑	❑	❑	❑
I take responsibility to turn in my homework.	❑	❑	❑	❑
I take responsibility to say "sorry" when I'm wrong.	❑	❑	❑	❑
Being responsible will help me do well in school.	❑	❑	❑	❑
I choose friends who are responsible.	❑	❑	❑	❑

He who excuses himself, accuses himself.

— *Gabriel Meurier*

Date:

Dear Parent/Guardian,

"I didn't do it!" or "It wasn't my fault!" These are phrases that teachers and parents hear often from kids. These phrases allow students to make excuses for their actions. The ability to admit wrongdoings and take responsibility for behavior is important for adults to model and for children to learn. Children of all ages need to have responsibility both at home and at school so they can practice this essential skill. In our next guidance lessons, we will be discussing the reasons is important to be responsible. Additionally, we will be discussing what responsibilities are expected at home and school. This would be a great time to discuss with your child the responsibilities you have as an adult and how your child's home responsibilities might change in the next year. Thank you, for helping your child understand the link between important life skills and school success.

Sincerely,

School Counselor

Activity 3.1

POETRY LINK

RESPONSIBILITY FROM START TO FINISH

Overview: Students will understand the importance of taking responsibility to complete tasks.

ASCA Indicator:
C:A2.8 Understand the importance of responsibility, dependability, punctuality, integrity and effort in the workplace

Materials: poem *From Start to Finish* page 73, Worksheet 3.1

Procedures:

1. Read the poem on page 73.
2. Discuss the importance of finishing tasks.
3. Distribute worksheet 3.1
4. Tell students to draw a picture of a career professional who has a job that they haven't completed: for instance a hair stylist who gave someone half of a haircut.
5. On the bottom of the worksheet, students need to write a sentence describing the importance of completing tasks.
6. Discuss the following questions:
   - How do people feel when a doctor or hair stylist or teacher doesn't finish a job?
   - What are things that teachers might get upset about if students don't finish?
   - What are some chores that parents would get upset if children didn't finish?
   - What steps can students take to improve responsibility in finishing tasks?
7. Teacher or counselor can create a bulletin board called "Why it's important to take responsibility to finish the job" and display the worksheets that students have completed.

RESPONSIBILITY FROM START TO FINISH

R responsibility

BY LISA KING

Finishing the job is important you see
In order to show off some responsibility.

You'd never find stylists doing half of "a do"
keeping half of it straight and half curly-q.

A builder won't put up only half of a wall
And a businessman won't hang up in the middle of a call.

And a teacher won't teach you half of the lesson
and rely on the students to just keep on guessin'.

No, all of these people will get their jobs done
In turn, you should too, it will help you a ton!

And so you should realize that finishing what you start
is important in math, in reading, and art.

So, start right away and then finish your work
it'll make you responsible (and teachers won't go berserk).

Worksheet 3.1

Name________________________

Draw a picture of someone who is on the job and only completes half of their work. On the bottom of the page, write a sentence about why it's important to make sure we are responsible to complete tasks.

It's important to take responsibility to complete a job because____________

____

____

____

Activity 3.2

STORY CONNECTION

HOW DO YOU SPELL RESPONSIBILITY?

Overview: Students will understand the importance of taking responsibility for themselves and have the opportunity to brainstorm different things they are responsible for at home and school.

ASCA Indicator:
A:A1.5: Identify attitudes and behaviors, which lead to successful learning

Materials: Worksheet 3.2 (Responsibility acrostic worksheet), How do you Spell Responsibility story page 76

Procedures:

1. Read story *How do you Spell Responsibility?* to the class. (page 76)
2. Afterwards, discuss the following questions:
   - What are some examples of things that Billy did not take responsibly?
   - How could Billy improve taking responsibility?
   - What might Billy be able to accomplish if he becomes more responsible?
3. Tell the class that we learned how Billy loved the spelling bee, and now we will have our own. Tell everyone to stand up and that we will now have a Responsibility Bee (instead of a spelling bee).
4. Explain that in this activity we will be using the word responsibility (show the worksheet 78) and for each letter in the word, the student whose turn it is will need to tell us a responsibility that starts with that letter. For example, the first person has the letter R. An example might be "Read every night" or " Remember to take out the trash". Counselors can accept anything that makes sense. the next student thinks of a responsibility that starts with E. (Eat your vegetables, etc.) If a student can't think of one they can say pass and sit down. The next student then gets the same letter E until someone thinks of one.
5. The last kid(s) who have successfully thought of responsibilities to coincide with that letter are deemed "Responsibility Champions."
6. Distribute Responsibility Acrostic worksheet page 78. Explain to students that they will do the activity we just did, but each person completes their own. If they need help they can take responsibility to ask a neighbor or friends sitting near them.
7. Counselor or teacher can display these in a bulletin board display or in a self-made "How do you show responsibility" book.

Activity 3.2

HOW DO YOU SPELL RESPONSIBILITY?

STORY CONNECTION

It was a cold winter at Blackwell Elementary School, and Billy was getting antsy for spring to get here. The only thing he liked about the winter was that there were some of the fun activities at school. One of his favorite activities was the school spelling bee. Billy was very good at spelling and each year he came close to winning the spelling bee in his class. He wished more than anything that he could make it to the school-wide spelling bee.

Mr. Smart, his teacher knew how much Billy wanted to win the spelling bee, and Mr. Smart believed the Billy could do it. Mr. Smart pulled Billy into the hallway the week before the spelling bee. He told Billy "You have the ability to win, but you have to take responsibility to study." Billy got very excited about being responsible and studying every word on his study guide, but when he got home Billy didn't study. He was busy with video games and with talking on the phone to his friends and watching TV. Since he didn't study, when the spelling bee in his class got underway, Billy was disqualified on the second round of the class spelling bee. When Randi won the class spelling bee, Mr. Smart asked proudly. So Randi, did you study these words? "Of course," said Randi. Most of the time, Randi completed her work, got to school on time, and studied for tests. Billy whispered under his breath, "Good old Responsible Randi."

Randi was on Billy's soccer team too. She always came to practice on time, and tried her best even when she wasn't having a great day. Billy got tired and grouchy when he didn't get a goal. Randi and Billy were friends. She noticed that Billy was trying to blame others when he messed up and she wished she could help him see that he needed to take responsibility to show off how smart he was. One day at soccer, Randi noticed Billy starting off practice in an extremely grumpy mood. "Billy, you have to take responsibility for what you do and what you say too. You have to have a good attitude at school and at play. No one else can take that responsibility for you." Billy didn't know how Randi was so smart. She sounded like a parent or teacher…. but Randi always came out on top, so maybe she was on to something.

He started thinking about how many times that week he did not take responsibility for homework, arguments with friends, soccer mistakes, and chores at home. He thought about what Randi had said. If Billy took responsibility for things like chores at home, school work and responsibility to have a good attitude maybe he would come out on top too. Maybe next year he would even win the spelling bee.

Do you think Billy could change his ways? What things would he need to improve on?

Worksheet 3.2

Name ______________________________

Think about the ways that you show responsibility.
Next to each letter, list a responsible behavior that starts with that letter.

R ______________________________

E ______________________________

S ______________________________

P ______________________________

O ______________________________

N ______________________________

S ______________________________

I ______________________________

B ______________________________

I ______________________________

L ______________________________

I ______________________________

T ______________________________

Y ______________________________

Activity 3.3

WORD SEARCH
RESPONSIBILITY

Overview: Students will understand the importance of being a responsible group member.

ASCA Indicator:
C.C2.3 Learn to work cooperatively with others as a team member

Materials: Responsibility Word Search page 80

Procedures:

1. Ask students, "When you are part of a group and someone in the group doesn't do their part, what do you do?"
    - Raise your hand if you would try to help your teammate with their part.
    - Put your hands on your head if you give a dirty look to the group member who is not doing their part.
    - Wave your hands in the air if you yell at that person who is not doing their part.
2. Divide class into office groups (see page 12 for explanation of office groups).
3. Distribute one word search to each group.
4. Give each group the task to divide out who is going to find which word(s). Discussion questions:
    - Who in the group said "I'll do it" right away?
    - Who wanted to take responsibility?
    - Whose responsibly contributed to the team?
    - How did you react when the other teammates didn't take responsibility?

Activity 3.3

Name: ____________________

Directions: Your group will need to complete a word search and find all of the words below. Please assign a word to group members. That person will be responsible to find the word in the word search.

Who is responsible to find this word?

RESPONSIBLE	____________	GOALS	____________
TIME	____________	HELP	____________
PLANNING	____________	HOMEWORK	____________
ADMITTING	____________	OWNERSHIP	____________
CHORE	____________	JOB	____________
FRIENDS	____________	ORGANIZE	____________

L	E	V	U	X	R	J	S	U	A	T	O	V	J	E
C	H	O	R	E	F	D	G	B	D	I	K	B	M	Z
R	N	T	F	C	N	S	G	N	M	M	B	X	M	I
W	T	N	R	E	Q	H	F	O	I	E	G	R	S	N
Z	J	L	I	E	E	K	W	Z	T	N	B	O	J	A
K	G	R	J	L	S	N	Q	M	T	J	N	C	R	G
W	F	O	P	C	E	P	U	L	I	H	S	A	K	R
H	Y	P	A	R	O	S	O	G	N	E	K	Q	L	O
N	K	T	S	L	T	U	T	N	G	E	U	S	H	P
H	I	H	P	G	S	Y	A	X	S	M	U	V	K	K
B	I	K	R	O	W	E	M	O	H	I	J	C	P	E
P	F	E	U	F	H	N	E	C	Y	Z	B	R	G	X
G	T	N	O	W	K	L	R	M	F	I	A	L	I	A
G	T	B	J	R	J	U	R	S	Q	E	I	N	E	D
D	E	X	O	O	E	E	W	H	L	M	Z	I	K	V

Activity 3.4

1,2,3 ACTION ROLE PLAYS

RESPONSIBILITY

Overview: Students will act out situations where following through with responsibilities leads to natural consequences.

ASCA Indicator:
C:A2.8 Understand the importance of responsibility, dependability, punctuality, integrity and effort in the workplace

Materials: Role-play cards (pg 82)

Procedures:

1. Introduce the lesson by discussing the importance of responsibility.
2. Split the class into office groups (see explanation of office group pg 12)
3. Distribute a role-play card to each group. (Copy the role play cards on page 82) and counselor will assign a director in each group.
4. Explain to class that we will be in our office groups for only 10 minutes and the skits should be no more than one minute.
5. The Director's role is to oversee decision-making and help to direct the skit. A good director isn't bossy, but is there to oversee and help make decisions if there is an argument.
6. The Actors should practice and all students in the group should sit with their heads down in order to let the facilitator know the group is ready.
7. To begin the skit the facilitator will say, "1,2,3 Action" similar to a director would in Hollywood. Encourage the students to clap when you say action.
8. Practice "1,2,3 Action" (with everyone clapping in unison when "Action" is said.)
9. The Director from each office group introduces their group and the counselor leads the class in saying "1,2,3 Action" to signal the group to perform.
10. After the skits, the facilitator leads a discussion asking these questions:
    a. Is it easy to take responsibility to admit when you are wrong?
    b. What are three different types of responsibilities that we saw in these skits?
    c. What are some school or home responsibilities that you try to get out of?
    d. What are some responsibilities that you get frustrated when adults don't follow through with what they say they are going to do and then don't?
    e. What are some school responsibilities that teachers get frustrated with when students don't take?

Activity 3.4

ROLE PLAY CARDS

Small groups of students can practice these role-plays and then perform in front of the class to illustrate the importance of being on time.

Your class is walking down the hall and your teacher hears someone talking. She asks who did it and wants someone to take responsibility.

Responsibility Role Play Card #1

You forgot your homework at home even though you did it. You want your teacher to know you did your work, but also that you take responsibility for forgetting it.

Responsibility Role Play Card #2

You are a teacher and you promised your class an ice cream party that they earned. You forgot the ice cream at home. How do you explain this to the class?

Responsibility Role Play Card #3

You want to go out and play with friends on a sunny day after school. Your parents tell you to do homework and chores before playing. You talk aloud to yourself about the importance of being responsible.

Responsibility Role Play Card #4

You have been assigned to do a group project on the animals of the ocean. One person in the group was assigned to research "dolphins," but didn't do their part. The group discusses their feelings about responsibility.

Responsibility Role Play Card #5

A TV talk show host is late to work. Guests on the show are waiting for the host who is a half an hour late. The subject of this show is taking responsibility.

Responsibility Role Play Card #6

Activity 3.5

I TAKE RESPONSIBILITY FOR MYSELF

Overview: Students will learn a way to remind themselves to take responsibility and not blame others or make excuses.

ASCA Indicator:
A:A3.1 Take responsibility for their actions

Materials: ball that you write "responsibility" on, *David Gets in Trouble* by David Shannon with homemade cover you can tape on saying "________'s Class." *Taking Responsibility Or Not* on page 85, sign page 84.

Procedures:

1. Ask students, "What are some common excuses that students use when they don't do their homework?" You will get answers such as "I left it at home," etc

2. Tell students, "Sometimes we make excuses for our actions. Like in the hall, if the teacher asks who is talking students might say,'It wasn't me.' Sometimes students even make excuses even if it was their fault."

3. Tell class that you have a book about that. Read the book *David Gets in Trouble* (but make a sign that says __ 's class book of excuses). Read book.

4. Tell the class that their teacher would prefer if students would say, " I did and I'm sorry" if they make a mistake. Taking responsibility is an important way to show that you are a professional student.

5. Tell class they will learn a pledge of responsibility. Tell them that instead of putting your hand on your heart like the pledge of allegiance this is a pledge where you start with your finger in the air. Tell them to put the pointer in the air and then point to themselves and say, "I—take responsibility—for myself." (During this lesson, if the counselor hears anyone blame or say "He/she did that…" have them put their finger in the air and repeat the pledge " I take responsibility for myself."

6. Ask for a volunteer and have them come to the front of the class. Take out the ball and throw it to the student and tell them to say " I did it" regardless of if they catch it or drop it.

7. Have that student throw the ball to another student. They need to say " I did it" whether or not they drop it or not.

8. Discuss how sometimes saying " I did it" is difficult for some.

9. Distribute worksheet 3.5 to students. Have them write different excuses in the boxes. Have them choose one box to write "I did it" in colored marker and the excuses in pencil.

10. Hang Sign 3.5 in classroom as a reminder.

Sign 3.5

RESPONSIBILITY PLEDGE POSTER

I Take Responsibility For Myself

Worksheet 3.5

TAKING RESPONSIBILITY OR NOT?

responsibility R

Directions:

In each ❍ circle, write a phrase that you might say if you were taking responsibility.

In each ❑ square, write a phrase that someone might say as an excuse, instead of taking responsibility.

Chapter 3

Activity 3.6

RATE YOUR RESPONSIBILITY

Overview: Students will look at their levels of responsibilities in different aspects of their lives.

ASCA Indicators:
A:A3.1 Take responsibility for their actions

Materials: Reproducible Worksheet page 87

Procedures:

1. Introduce the word R E S P O N S I B I L I T Y by doing a game of hangman on the board until someone guesses this word. Ask if anyone can define this word. Tell that we will be discussing how responsible they are.

2. Distribute worksheet on the next page to students. Tell them to circle the appropriate number on the number line as to how responsible they think they are with this part of life. (10 being not at all responsible and 1 being very responsible)

3. Turn to a person beside you and compare one thing about your rating sheet. Discuss things you have in common about what your responsibilities are at home.

4. Tell them, "Close your eyes and imagine a single file line of your whole class. Image that the person in the front of the line was the most responsible. Don't say it out loud, but imagine that behind that person is the next most responsible person, then the next & at the end of the line would be the least responsible students. Where would you be in line?"

   Answer—need to set goals and work toward them

5. Discussion questions:

   a. What would you need to do to move up in line or to be more responsible?

   b. What is something you are very responsible about?

   c. What is something that is hard for you to take responsibility?

   d. What is something you and your partner had in common?

Worksheet 3.6

RATE YOUR RESPONSIBILITY

	Very Responsible									Not Responsible
Homework	1 ☺	2	3	4	5	6	7	8	9	10 ☹
Math	1 ☺	2	3	4	5	6	7	8	9	10 ☹
Getting Along With Friends	1 ☺	2	3	4	5	6	7	8	9	10 ☹
Getting Along With Family	1 ☺	2	3	4	5	6	7	8	9	10 ☹
Reading	1 ☺	2	3	4	5	6	7	8	9	10 ☹
PE	1 ☺	2	3	4	5	6	7	8	9	10 ☹
Behavior At School	1 ☺	2	3	4	5	6	7	8	9	10 ☹
Studying For Tests	1 ☺	2	3	4	5	6	7	8	9	10 ☹
Music	1 ☺	2	3	4	5	6	7	8	9	10 ☹
Doing Chores	1 ☺	2	3	4	5	6	7	8	9	10 ☹
Art	1 ☺	2	3	4	5	6	7	8	9	10 ☹
Going To Bed On Time	1 ☺	2	3	4	5	6	7	8	9	10 ☹

Activity 3.7

RESPONSIBILITY FOUR CORNERS

Overview: Through a game of four corners, the student will understand age appropriate responsibilities and realistic academic goals. The student will examine their perception of their own responsibilities.

ASCA Indicators:
A:B2.1 Establish challenging goals in elementary middle, and high school.

C:A2.8 Understand the importance of responsibility, dependability, punctuality, integrity and effort in the workplace

Materials: 4 corners signs (pages 89-92), Scotch tape

Procedures:

1. Hang the four signs (89-92) in the four corners of the classroom. Ask the class if anyone knows what responsibility means?
2. Explain rules of the game. Say," When I say go, you will stand up and listen to the sentence that I say, for example "I make my bed." You will go to the corner that describes you. Do you take this responsibility always, sometimes, often or never? Please take responsibility to walk quietly and without running." Remind students to take responsibility for themselves and not their friends .
3. Say the following sentences and discuss as needed. I take responsibility to: (students go to appropriate corner for):
   - Make my bed.
   - Start my homework without reminders.
   - Turn in my homework on time.
   - To set the table
   - For cleaning up the table
   - For not calling out in class
   - For studying for spelling tests.
   - For paying for the electric bill at my house
   - I take responsibility for my choices
   - I take responsibility to say sorry when I am wrong
   - (say this as the last one)—I take responsibility to come to school with all my clothes on.
4. After the last statement, say "Now take responsibility to walk quietly back to your seat." Discuss that students tend to take responsibility for things important to you. Give an example that it is important for students to come to school with their clothes so they do it, just like they take responsibility to remember when their favorite TV show is on. Discuss that when they do not take responsibility to do something they are telling the person it is not important. (for example when you don't turn in homework or don't apologize to a friend.)
5. Discussion Questions:
   - Did you find yourself in one corner most of the time?
   - Do you wish that you would be in different corners (or be more responsible)
   - Do you think if we did this activity next year you will go to the same corners?
   - How could you make a plan to improve your responsibility?
   - Did you learn anything about yourself or about ____ graders in general?

Worksheet 3.7A

Chapter 3

Worksheet 3.7B

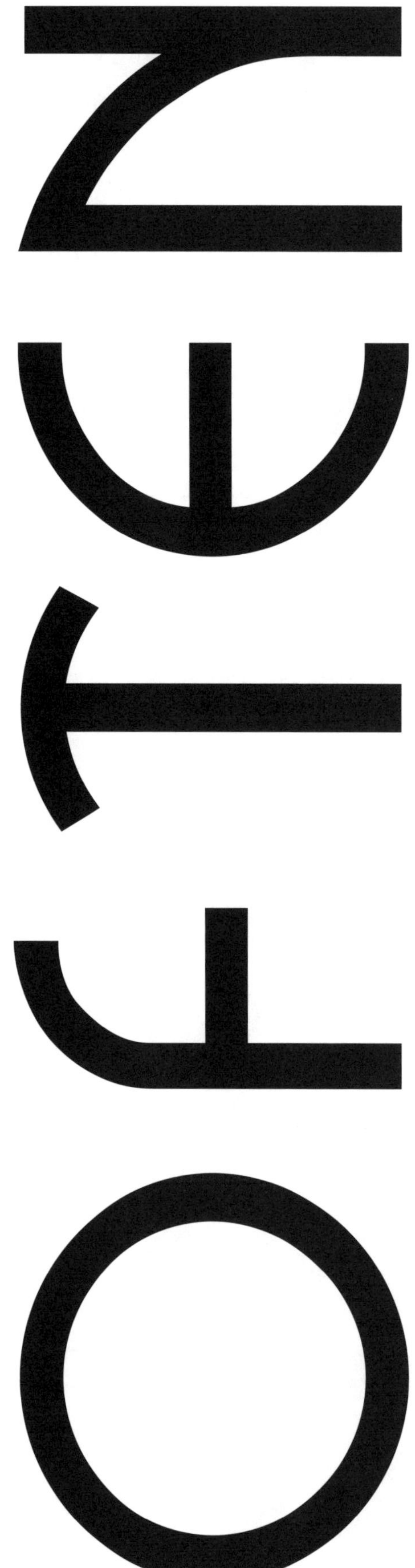

Worksheet 3.7C

SOMETIMES

Chapter 3

Worksheet 3.7D

Chapter 4

LEARNING FROM MISTAKES

Chapter 4

Everyone makes mistakes. This chapter includes lessons that help students understand that mistakes are a normal part of the learning process. It's important for students to realize that their friends, family and even teachers make mistakes. As long as you are trying your hardest, it is absolutely OK… even expected that you will sometimes mess up. If you didn't mess up you wouldn't know what NOT to do.

Indicators from ASCA National Model that are addressed in this chapter (see crosswalk pg 21):

A:A2.3 ....Use communication skills to know when and how to ask for help when needed.

A:A1.4 ....Accept mistakes as essential to the learning process

A:A1.5 ....Identify attitudes and behaviors, which lead to successful learning

A:A3.1 ....Take responsibility for their actions

Chapter Contents

PRE-POST SURVEY
FOR LEARNING FROM MISTAKES

Overview: To assess student perception on learning from mistakes.

ASCA Indicator:
A:A1.4 Accept mistakes as essential to the learning process

Materials Needed:
Learning from Mistakes Survey

Procedures:

1. Distribute Learning from Mistakes Survey before the lesson(s) you intend to do on time management.
2. Compile the results to give you an idea of how the group/class feels about time management and their perceptions.
3. Repeat the survey at the end of the lesson(s) to assess what the students have improved on and how perceptions have changed.

Learning From Mistakes Survey

	True	False
Adults don't make many mistakes because they have learned how to avoid mistakes.	❑	❑
When I mess up, I am a failure.	❑	❑
Everyone in the world makes mistakes.	❑	❑
I need to get everything correct in order for my teacher to think I am smart.	❑	❑
If I don't understand what to do, I should ask so that I don't make a mistake.	❑	❑
I am worried about making mistakes.	❑	❑
It is respectful to laugh quietly when others make mistakes.	❑	❑
It is Ok to laugh at your own mistakes as long as your mistake didn't hurt anyone.	❑	❑

An error doesn't become a mistake until you refuse to correct it.

— Anonymous

Date:

Dear Parent/Guardian,

Everyone makes mistakes, which of course is how we learn. It's important for students to realize that their friends, family and teachers make mistakes. As long as you are trying your hardest, it is absolutely OK … even expected that you will sometimes mess up. If you didn't mess up you wouldn't know what NOT to do. As adults, it is common for us to make mistakes in front of kids. It is important to make some of these instances learning experiences so that our kids can see us model a positive way to handle mistakes. We will soon be doing a lesson on learning from mistakes, and accepting mistakes as a natural consequence in the path of acquiring new skills. It would be a great time to have a family discussion about how the adults in your home handle mistakes. Thank you for helping your child understand the link between important life skills and school success.

Sincerely,

School Counselor

Activity 4.1

POETRY LINK

LEARNING FROM MISTAKES

Overview: This lesson gives students a real experience to monitor how they react when they make mistakes.

ASCA Indicator:
A: A1.4 Accept mistakes as essential to the learning process

Materials: Poem (page 97), Poem cards (page 98)

Procedures:

1. Read poem to class or group.
2. Divide the class into groups of three or four students per group.
3. Distribute the poem cards (page 98) to each group and tell them that they will have to memorize their lines and perform the poem. They will have 6 minutes to learn the lines and practice in their groups. Tell the class that in this lesson we will be testing people's memory.
4. Allow groups to have approximately 6 minutes to memorize the lines of the poem. Have the groups perform their stanza of the poem if they can.
5. When the groups have all attempted to say their part, discuss the following questions:
   - How many people got frustrated when they messed up?
   - What are some other feelings you had?
   - What was this poem about?
   - This lesson really isn't about memory. What do you think this lesson is trying to teach?

LEARNING FROM MISTAKES

BY LISA KING

Who me? Not me! It couldn't be
I never make mistakes you see

It must have been Henry or Dwight
They're often wrong. I'm always right!

Uh-Oh. For real? You really say
It's me who did it wrong today?

Oh drat! I goofed—I'm incorrect.
My answer's not what you expect.

Wait a sec—you understand
That sometimes I might need a hand!

Now I get it. Now I see—
Next time I'll do it error free!

Mistakes occur at every turn—
But that's OK—that's how we learn!

Activity 4.1

Small groups of students can practice these role-plays and then perform in front of the class to illustrate the importance of being on time.

Who me? Not me!
It couldn't be
I never make mistakes
You see

Poem Card #1

It must have been
Henry or Dwight
They're often wrong.
I'm always right!

Poem Card #2

Uh Oh. For real?
You really say
It's me who
Did it wrong today?

Poem Card #3

Oh drat! I goofed—
I'm incorrect.
My answer's not
what you expect.

Poem Card #4

Wait a sec—
You understand
That sometimes
I might need a hand!

Poem Card #5

Now I get it.
Now I see—
Next time I'll do
It error free!

Poem Card #6

Mistakes occur
At every turn—
But that's OK—
That's how we learn!

Poem Card #7

Activity 4.2

STORY CONNECTION

EVERYONE MAKES MISTAKES DEER

Overview: Through this activity students will see how mistakes help the learning process.

ASCA Indicators:

A: A1.4 Accept mistakes as essential to the learning process

A:A1.5: Identify attitudes and behaviors, which lead to successful learning

A:A3.1 Take responsibility for their actions

Materials: *Everyone makes mistakes deer* story (page 100), Deer puppet (optional), Activity 4.2, Poster 4.2

Procedures:

1. Divide class in to partners (groups of three would work too).
2. Tell students that we are taking about mistakes today. We will first do a survey of the class to see what we have in common about this subject.
3. We will do a thumbs up, thumbs down activity. I will read a statement and if you have done this, put your thumbs up and if you haven't done this put your thumbs down.
   a. I have made a mistake before. (Everyone should have their thumbs up!)
   b. I have called my teacher "mom."
   c. I have gotten lost.
   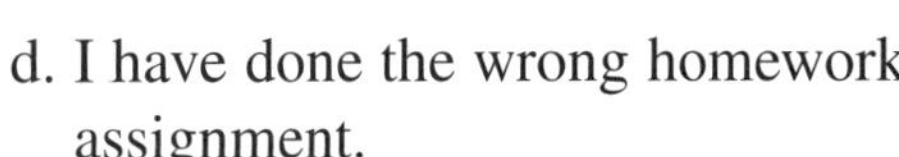
   d. I have done the wrong homework assignment.
   e. I have dialed the wrong number on the telephone.
   f. I have walked into the wrong bathroom.
   g. I have gone to hold the hand of an adult I thought was my parent, and it was a stranger.
4. Now we see that everyone makes mistakes. "It's Ok… everyone makes mistakes, dear." Has anyone ever said that to you? Sometimes your mom or teacher might call you sweetie or dear. Read the story to the class. (use deer finger puppet as option)
5. Divide class into partner groups and distribute one copy of Activity 4.2 to each group.
6. Tell class we will have a coloring contest and that each partner group will turn in one sheet. You only have 5 minutes. Work quickly and if your partner messes up tell them, "Everyone makes mistakes, deer."
7. Display Poster 4.2 in class.

Activity 4.2

EVERYONE MAKES MIS-TAKES DEER

STORY CONNECTION

There once was a deer with a very strange name that taught children important lessons. This deer's name was long and unusual. His first name was "Everyone." Everyone Deer had a mission in life that suited his full name. His mission and purpose was to help boys and girls remember that no one is perfect. By now you might be curious as to what his middle name is. This deer had two middle names and they were Makes Mistakes. Teachers and parents often used him as an example when teaching that no one is perfect. Teachers can often be heard telling others "Everyone Makes Mistakes." Sometimes they include his last name too and they say "Everyone Makes Mistakes Deer." If you listen, you can hear people spreading this deer's message when they or their friends mess up.

The story that's been passed down is that Everyone Deer has appeared at different times throughout the past few decades and he reminds kids not to be so hard on themselves. For example in 1973, there was a boy named Michael who was a star pitcher on his high school baseball team. One day, he had his best game ever and struck out nine batters. For some reason, in the games after that big win, he started making many mistakes. He would get so frustrated with his mistakes, that he made even more mistakes. He began a slump that lasted for the next six games. Toward the end of the season, Michael and his team had a game in the countryside. Michael started to get mad at himself when the first batter hit a homerun. He felt like stomping off the mound. Suddenly in the outfield he saw a deer running toward him. Michael didn't think it was that strange because they were in the country, but the strange thing was that he thought he heard the deer talk. He thought he heard the deer say, " Everyone makes mistakes. Don't be so hard on yourself!"

Years later, Everyone Makes Mistakes Deer showed up again.

What do you think Michael learned from Everyone Deer?

____

____

____

Where do you think Everyone Makes Mistakes Deer showed up?

____

____

____

Activity 4.2

COLORING CONTEST

Name ____________________

You will have 3 minutes to participate in this coloring contest.

E_ _ _ _ _ _ _ _ _ M_ _ _ _ _

_ _ _ _ _ _K_ _ DEER

Poster 4.2

EVERYONE MAKES MISTAKES DEER

REMINDS US THAT:

1. There is a difference between not following the rules and making mistakes when you are trying your best.

2. Goofs can be Lessons!

3. Mistakes are made so that we can learn.

4. Don't let messing up go to your head!

5. Everyone makes mistakes, dear!

Worksheet 4.3

WORD SEARCH

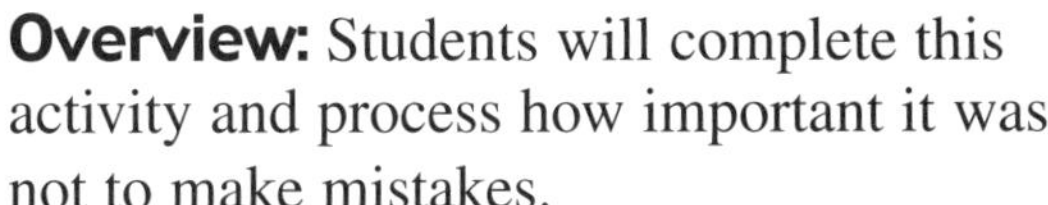

Overview: Students will complete this activity and process how important it was not to make mistakes.

ASCA Indicator:
A:A1.4 Accept mistakes as essential to the learning process

A:A1.5: Identify attitudes and behaviors, which lead to successful learning

Materials Needed:
Pen or markers, Word Search (page 104)

Procedures:

1. Distribute word search to students.
2. Tell the class that we will start this lesson with a contest to see how many words you can find in this word search. The only rules are that you have 4 minutes and that you have to use a pen or marker. Remind them in this game it's speed that counts, so mark the word as soon as you see it.
3. After four minutes, have the students put their pens down.
4. Tell students that this was a different kind of contest. At the bottom of the page:
   - For #1, write how many words you found.
   - For #2, write how many mistakes you made (how many stray marks)

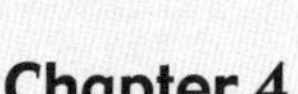

Activity 4.3

Name: ____________________________

ASK	DIFFICULT
EVERYONE	HELP
LEARN	QUESTION
MISTAKE	PROBLEM
PERFECTION	RESPONSIBILITY
OOPS	UNDERSTAND

It's Ok to make a mistake
in this Word Search

1. How many did you find?__________
2. ____________

S E O G J H I A Q U R M Z L W
P K N O D F S U D N Y I R H O
E E B O P K E C F D E S O F O
M I R P Y S O T O E K T H L P
U Y P F T R Z N L R A A Q L T
X R O I E R E O V S T K A V H
K W O J T C V V D T S F H U M
L N K G B L T C E A I F E E E
S J S L P E K I H N M U L S U
P U F C M V H M O D I B P G E
T L U C I F F I D N O P C W V
L E A R N J P F W R D E L I X
Y C R W K O B I P W A O D P S
R E S P O N S I B I L I T Y W
K S X E M I S T K K E C K D E

Activity 4.4

1, 2, 3, ACTION ROLE PLAYS

Overview: Students will act out situations where mistakes lead to learning.

ASCA Indicator:
A: A1.4 Accept mistakes as essential to the learning process

Materials: Role-play cards (pg 106)

Procedures:

1. Introduce the lesson by asking how many people have made a mistake this week? Tell the class that we will be examining how mistakes are part of the learning process.
2. Split the class into office groups (see explanation of office group pg 12) and assign a Director in each group.
3. Distribute a role-play card to each group. (Copy the role play cards on page 106)
4. Explain to class that we will be in our office groups for only 10 minutes and the skits should be no more than one minute.
5. The Director's role is to oversee decision-making and help to direct the skit. A good director isn't bossy, but is there to oversee and help make decisions if there is an argument.
6. The students who will act out the skits should practice and all students in the group should sit with their heads down when they are ready to let the facilitator know the group is ready.
7. To begin the skit the facilitator will say, "1,2,3 Action" similar to a director would in Hollywood movie. Encourage the students to clap when you say action.
8. Tell the students that in these skits, we will see how people have different feelings when they make mistakes.
9. The Director from the first office group introduces their group and the counselor leads the class in saying "1,2,3 Action" to signal the group to perform. Subsequently, other groups perform.
10. After the skits, the facilitator leads a discussion asking these questions:
    - What were the different feelings people had after making mistakes?
    - How do you react when you make a mistake?
    - What are some things people can do to make things better when a mistake is made?
    - Why are mistakes important to learning?

Activity 4.4

ROLE PLAY CARDS
LEARNING FROM MISTAKES

Small groups of students can practice these role-plays and then perform in front of the class to illustrate the importance of learning from their mistakes.

You raised your hand to answer a question and you get it wrong. You get embarrassed and laugh it off. When you tell your mom about it, she says some words to make you feel better.

Mistakes Role Play Card #1

One student does an assignment wrong. He/she does the odd problems instead of the even problems. She gets worried that the teacher will get mad.

Mistakes Role Play Card #2

You are working on a group project and one of your group members did not do their part in the project. The person tries to say, "It wasn't my fault!" The rest of the group gets mad. How can you explain to that student the difference between a mistake and a responsibility.

Mistakes Role Play Card #3

You forget your homework at home, but actually had done it. It truly was a mistake. You are frustrated with yourself. How do you explain it to the teacher? Does the teacher believe you?

Mistakes Role Play Card #4

You accidentally forget your friend's birthday. You are really sorry. How can you explain your mistake to your friend?

Mistakes Role Play Card #5

A scientist discovers something by accident, but his invention has a great purpose (you decide if the invention is a medicine, a toy, or something else). The research group is excited that after many tries, your research group learned from trying all these years.

Mistakes Role Play Card #6

Activity 4.5

MISTAKES THAT WORKED

Overview: Students will look at real life examples of how mistakes can sometimes be useful.

ASCA Indicator:
A: A1.4 Accept mistakes as essential to the learning process

Materials: Deer puppet, silly putty, potato chips, chocolate chip cookies, coke, slinky, book *Mistakes that Worked* by Charlotte Foltz Jones

Procedure:

1. To introduce today's lesson let's play a game. Follow these directions:
    - Stand up if you have ever misspelled a word.
    - Put your hands on your head if you have ever been lost.
    - Put your hands in the air if you have ever called your teacher mom.
    - Put your hands on your toes if you ever thought you messed up on an art project.
    - Wave to me if you think that mistakes can be useful.
2. All of these things are mistakes and everyone makes mistakes. Today we will be talking about all kinds of mistakes such as potato chips, slinkies, and silly putty, which are all mistakes!
3. Explain that sometimes when people work hard and end up making a mistake, it actually can turn into a useful thing.
4. Tell the class that we will now read about some common things that actually were discovered by mistakes. (If you have the book *Mistakes that Worked* by Jones, show the book to the class).
5. Allow students to choose a "Mistakes that Worked" Card (page 108). If someone makes a mistake while reading and gets a word wrong remember not to laugh but think in your head, "everyone makes mistakes."

Activity 4.5A

MISTAKES THAT WORKED CARDS
(FRONT OF CARD)

Chocolate Chip Cookies

Mistake Card #1

Potato Chips

Mistake Card #2

Silly Putty

Mistake Card #4

SLINKY

Mistake Card #3

Coca-Cola

Mistake Card #5

Velcro

Mistake Card #6

Activity 4.5B

MISTAKES THAT WORKED CARDS
(BACK OF CARD)

1930—Ruth Wakefield worked at a bakery where she always made chocolate cookies. One day, she didn't have any bakers chocolate to make these chocolate cookies. She tried to fix her **mistake** by breaking semi-sweet chocolate into bits. She thought the bits would melt throughout the dough. She meant to make chocolate cookies, but by **mistake**, she invented the chocolate chip cookie.

1944—During World War II the United States government needed rubber for airplane tires. A scientist named James Wright tried to make this rubber when he added a chemical, which made the rubber too sticky. He made the **mistake** of making a rubber that couldn't be used for tires. But someone thought of the idea to sell this rubber as a toy called silly putty.

1853—A chef named George Crum worked at a restaurant in New York. One day, a customer complained about his fried potatoes and sent his plate back to the kitchen. He wanted his potatoes sliced thinner. The chef made the potatoes as thin and crispy as possible to try to annoy the customer, but the customer loved them. His potatoes are now known as potato chips.

1886—A man named Dr. Pemberton was making a health tonic to help stress and headaches. He took it to Jacob's Pharmacy and told Jacob to add water and ice to the tonic. Jacob made the **mistake** of putting in carbonated water instead of regular water. After tasting the mixture they decided it should be a fountain drink. The name Coca-Cola was given to the drink because it contained cocoa leaves and cola-nuts.

1943—During World War II, Richard James was on a new ship. As he worked on the ship's machines, he saw a spring fall to the floor and wiggle from side to side. When he got back home, he remembered the spring that popped out by **mistake**. Richard and his wife Betty started making a spring as a toy in America called the slinky.

1948—A man arrived home from a walk and by **mistake** had collected the sticky burs from a plant on his jacket. The cockleburs that were stuck to him and his clothing gave him an idea. He thought this would be a good new way to fasten things. After eight years of experiments he made VELCRO.

Activity 4.6

LITERATURE LINK
USING POSITIVE SELF-TALK

Overview: When kids make mistakes, often they get angry. This lesson teaches students a strategy to deal with mistakes by changing negative thoughts to positive thoughts.

ASCA Indicator:
A:A1.4 Accept mistakes as essential to the learning process

Materials: Pieces of construction paper with different anger management strategies written on them (i.e.punch a pillow, deep breath, count to 10, talk to a friend), *Moe the Dog in Tropical Paradise* by Diane Stanley, blank cassette and tape recorder

Procedures:

1. Ask the class what they do to calm down if they get mad when they make a mistake. Review anger management strategies(i.e. punch a pillow, deep breath, count to 10, talk to a friend).
2. Tell the class that there is a new strategy we will be learning today. Tell them "I will model a situation with a student where I get angry using this new anger management strategy called self-talk." Explain that self-talk is where we tell ourselves things in our heads. Positive self-talk, helps us.
3. Select a student to act like the teacher and ask what is 2+2. I answer 3. And the teacher corrects me. I then will pretend to be the student doing self-talk out loud saying "It's Ok, next time I'll get it." Tell the class that this is an example of how we can use positive self-talk. Repeat the role-play but this time model negative self-talk saying, "Man, I'm so stupid I always get things wrong."
4. Take out cassette recorder. Tell them that self-talk is like a cassette tape or CD in your head that plays over and over. Sometimes we have to record over the negative self-talk with positive self-talk.
5. Press record and the counselor will say a negative thought. Then press stop. Allow a student to change that thought into positive self-talk and record them saying the positive statement into the recorder. At the end of the following statements play the tape back for the class.
6. Discuss how students and professionals use self-talk as an important strategy.

Variations:

- Have students be detectives looking for self-talk. Let the students practice showing a thumbs up when they hear positive self-talk and thumbs down for negative self-talk. Read *Moe the Dog in Tropical Paradise* and have them do thumbs up and thumbs down when they hear self-talk.
- Read *The Very Angry Day that Amy Didn't Have* and review positive and negative self-talk.
- Practice self-talk while looking in a hand mirror. Pass it around the class so that students can practice.

Activity 4.7

ASK FOR HELP WHEN NEEDED

Materials: Worksheet on 4.7 "Asking for Help," *Ali Ask for Help* story below

Procedures:

1. Read the following situation:

   Ali Ask for Help lived in a small swamp in a small town. He was a smart alligator, and always seemed to know what was going on. He could figure out most things on his own, but when he got confused he always asked for help. This was how he stayed on top of things. One day his sister Alyse Alligator sat on a swamp stone and cried because she didn't understand her homework. Ali slithered over and waited in the water until Alyse said, "Why are you just swimming there? Don't you want to help?" Ali explained that he didn't know what was wrong. He said, "Alyse, I can't assume I know what is, wrong. You have to let me know what kind of help you need. Asking for help is important when you are confused."

2. Tell the students that since we have been talking about listening skills, you are going to give a quiz about the story to see if they were listening. Hand out Worksheet 4.7 on page 112. Put it on the students' desk face down.

3. Have them begin when you say, "Ready, set, go." *(Note: The point of this exercise is that the worksheet has no directions and no true way to know what to do. We hope the students have learned to ask for help since they cannot know what to do.)*

4. When the first student raises their hand to ask what to do, tell the class to put their pencils down and reward that student with a small treat.

5. Explain that the reason the person was rewarded is because he/she asked for help when needed which is an important skill. There were no directions and no way to know what to.

6. Have students cease doing the 'quiz' independently.

7. Now, have students ask if anyone has questions on #1. (if needed, prompt the audience to raise their hands and ask, "What do you do on #1?")

8. Tell students "On Number one, the question asks, 'What is 2+2?'"

9. If there is time, you can have a student to come up for each number on the worksheet and pretend they are the teacher. They can make up what the question should be for the answers on Worksheet 4.7. (For instance, when someone asks what to do on #3, the "teacher" can say draw a frown face next to the smiley face and for #6 the teacher can decide what to draw in the box.)

10. After 1-6 is completed, #7 should be filled in "Ask for help when you need it!"

Worksheet 4.7

ASK FOR HELP WHEN NEEDED

Name: ______________________________

1. 2 2 =
2. 4 1 =
3. ☺
4. c____t
5. t____p

6. Draw the picture here:

7. The lesson is:

____

____

____

Chapter 5

TEST-TAKING SKILLS

Chapter 5

School is a place where students learn and grow. Tests, quizzes and other measures of evaluation are a regular part of a student's life, as a teacher needs to determine what a student has learned. It is important to prepare students as best we can to be able to have the test readiness skills they need to perform their best. In this chapter, there are lessons and activities to help students learn, review and understand the importance of test taking skills.

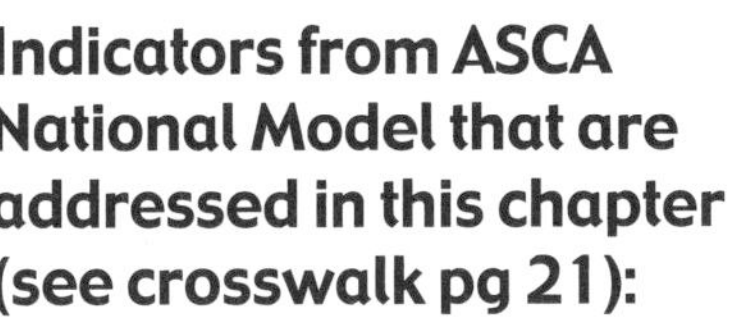

Indicators from ASCA National Model that are addressed in this chapter (see crosswalk pg 21):

A:A1.5 ....Identify attitudes and behaviors, which lead to successful learning.

A:A2.2 ....Demonstrate how effort and persistence positively affect learning.

A:A3.1 ....Take responsibility for their actions.

A:A3.4 ....Demonstrate dependability, productivity and initiative.

A:B2.6......Understand the relationship between classroom performance and success in school.

C.C2.3......Learn to work cooperatively with others as a team member.

PS-A1.8....Understand the need for self-control and how to practice.

Chapter Contents

PRE-POST SURVEY
FOR TEST-TAKING SKILLS

Overview: To assess student perception on taking tests. This pre-post survey can be used in classroom guidance or for a small group.

ASCA Indicator:
A:A1.5: Identify attitudes and behaviors which lead to successful learning.

Materials Needed:
Time Management Survey

Procedures:

1. Distribute Test-Taking Survey before the lesson(s) you intend to do on testing skills.
2. Compile the results to give you an ideas of how the group/class feels about time management.
3. Repeat the survey at the end of the lesson(s) to assess what the students have improved on and how perceptions have changed.

Student Survey on Test Taking

	Strongly Agree	Agree	Disagree	Strongly Disagree
I must study for standardized tests.	❑	❑	❑	❑
Before a test I usually eat a good breakfast.	❑	❑	❑	❑
It is important to finish first on a test.	❑	❑	❑	❑
I try to get a good night of sleep before a test.	❑	❑	❑	❑
I get stressed about tests.	❑	❑	❑	❑
I like taking tests.	❑	❑	❑	❑

Learning is not a spectator sport.

— Anonymous

Date:

Dear Parent/Guardian,

Students often feel the pressure of a big test. As young people are learning to deal with testing, it is important to make sure that students are equipped with the skills to deal with test anxiety. Additionally, it is vital for students to know how to appropriately prepare for a big test. In our guidance lessons, students will be learning important study skills, test preparation skills, and ways to decrease test anxiety. This would be a great time to introduce a family discussion about the importance of getting a good night rest, eating a healthy breakfast and being prepared for tests. Certainly students sometimes dread testing experiences, so it is important to prepare students to do their best. Thank you for helping your child understand the link between important life skills and school success.

Sincerely,

School Counselor

Activity 5.1

POETRY LINK

TEST STRESS

Overview: Students will examine test anxiety and learn ways to overcome the stress that can go along with testing situations.

ASCA Indicator:

A:A1.5 Identify attitudes and behaviors, which lead to successful learning

A:B2.6 Understand the relationship between classroom performance and success in school

Materials: Poem page 117, Checklist in Worksheet 5.1A, Worksheet 5.1B, crayons

Procedures:

1. Read the poem to the class.
2. Ask the students to follow these directions:
   - Stand up if you get nervous on tests
   - Stand up if you get excited on tests
3. Discuss how it is possible to have more than one feeling at the same time. Compare this to the feeling of being on a roller coaster. It is both exciting and scary.
4. Ask the class, "What is test anxiety? What happens to our bodies when we get test anxiety?"
   - ***physically***—butterflies in stomach, sweaty palms, jittery, tense, nausea, sleeplessness
   - ***psychologically***—worry about what will happen, blank out, panic
5. Discuss with the class that humans have a panic response that lets our bodies know to be on guard when we get stressed. You need to diffuse your body's panic response. Train it to remain calm when presented with tests. First, stop putting so much weight on the exam.
6. Ask the students to think of ways they could reduce stress while taking a test.
7. Have the checklist (page 18) available for students who experience test anxiety. Explain how to use this checklist with the entire class and leave some checklists for those who are interested.

Variations:

- Read *Thomas's Sheep and the Great Geography Test* by Steven L. Layne, which is about a boy who is worried about an upcoming geography test. Thomas finds himself unable to fall asleep until he uses a useful strategy of counting sheep.
- Draw a silhouette of a body and color in the parts of the body that feel test stress. Label what the body is feeling on Worksheet 5.1.

TEST STRESS

BY TRACI KING

I cannot think
My mind's astray
I have a great big test today.

I've studied lots
I am prepared.
But, oh my goodness, now I'm scared.

Multiple Choice
A or B?
My mind is blank, how can this be?

I cannot do it.
I think I'll fail.
I'll never ever get into Yale.

But wait.
I'm ready.
I have prepared.
There is no reason to be scared.

I've rested lots.
I know this stuff.
Reviewed my notes more than enough.

I'll take my time,
And do my best
and then I know I'll ace this test.

Worksheet 5.1A

TEST STRESS CHECKLIST

Directions:
If you experience test anxiety, use this checklist to make sure you decrease your stress.

- ❑ I practice taking relaxing deep breaths.
- ❑ I have my materials organized for the test (watch, pen/pencils, paper, calculator)
- ❑ I need to eat a light meal before the test.
- ❑ I need a good night of sleep before the test.
- ❑ I get to school on time.
- ❑ I imagine I am doing my best on the exam. I can see myself looking over the test, writing answers, and feeling calm.
- ❑ I avoid talking nervously to people prior to the test.
- ❑ If I start to feel nervous, I will put my pencil down and make calming, positive statements while practicing my relaxation for a minute or so.
- ❑ I can complete a practice test complete with a quiet room, a classroom type desk and a time limit.
- ❑ I share my nervous feelings with someone.
- ❑ I have made a list of at least two confidence-building statements and practice saying them to myself regularly.

These positive statements are:

1. ______________________________

2. ______________________________

Worksheet 5.1B

TEST STRESS

Directions: Color in the areas that you feel stress in your body. Choose one color and color lightly where you feel lighter stress and color darker where you feel more intense stress.

Chapter 5

Ways that I can reduce stress:

1. ______________________________

2. ______________________________

3. ______________________________

Activity 5.2

STORY CONNECTION

KNOW IT ALL

Overview: Through this short story students will be reminded of the test preparations skills.

ASCA Indicator:
A:A1.5 Identify attitudes and behaviors, which lead to successful learning

Materials: Know it All Story (pages 121-124 cut and fastened together as a book), Bingo cards for each student (page 125), bingo chips (math counters will work)

Procedures:

1. Review test taking tips that the students already know.
2. Read *Know it All* story.
3. Distribute Test Taking Bingo Cards to class. Have students use the phrases in the box at the bottom of the page to create their own bingo card.
4. Tell class that they need four in a row to get Bingo and to win they need to stand and say "Test Taking Bingo"
5. After the first round of bingo, have the class make up a rap like Johnny did. You can have groups make up a class rap/cheer with motions, using some of the phrases in the box on the bottom of page 122.
6. Have group or class perform the rap with motions. Do the rap/cheer with the motions but no words. Encourage the teacher to have them do this as a stretch break on test days.
7. Play another round of test taking bingo. Do the rap/cheer for winner.

Activity 5.2

KNOW IT ALL
STORY CONNECTION

Cover

At Blackwood Elementary School, Mr. Smart's class had twenty-three students. Each student was different. Some were tall, some short, some liked math, and some liked reading best. Johnny liked all the subjects in school. In fact, he was a very smart kid. When he got an answer correct he always bragged about it. In fact, he was a real know-it-all. Johnny thought he knew everything. When he was right, he wasn't shy about telling you ALL about it. " I knew it!" or "Told you so," he would say.

Page 1

Activity 5.2

KNOW IT ALL

STORY CONNECTION

One day, Johnny's teacher, Mr. Smart announced that there was a big test coming up. Johnny was all smiles. He loved tests and made sure to pay attention when he heard that magic word… test. Mr. Smart announced that this test was a special kind of test called a standardized test. Mr. Smart asked, "Does anyone know the name of the test we will be taking?" Johnny answered " It's the _________." Mr. Smart explained that this was correct and this was a chance for students to show their teachers and parents how smart they were. Johnny was excited, "Told you so" he said to Dylan who sat next to him.

In the next week, Mr. Smart mentioned the test a lot. He kept saying not to worry, but he made the class practice a lot for the test. The counselor, Mrs. Prince, came to the class and told the students, "I will teach you everything you need to know for the test." Johnny couldn't wait and listened to every word she said. They learned the art of bubbling in circles, about how important sleep is, eating a good breakfast and about trying your best on a test. Mrs. Prince told us to pay attention as she wrote a question on the board. "On the day of the test you should: a) come to school an hour early b) come on time c) come an hour late. She drew bubbles on the board beside each letter and filled in the letter b. "Told you so" said Johnny.

Page 2

The homework that night was to tell your parents about how to take a test. Johnny went all out and actually made up a rap to remember everything he needed to know. "Eat a good breakfast, get lots of rest, don't be tardy, DO YOUR BEST!" He even made up motions to go with the testing rhyme.

Page 3

(allow students to show what motions they think he used and repeat rap)

Activity 5.2

KNOW IT ALL
STORY CONNECTION

The next day he was ready to share his rhyme and show off to Mr. Smart. But Mr. Smart said, “Not now Johnny, there is no talking, it’s time for the test.” The class had to sit quietly as Mr. Smart passed out the No. 2 pencils and started reading directions. Johnny was not tuned in to what was going on and he was singing his song to himself, “Eat a good breakfast, get lots of rest, don’t be tardy, DO YOUR BEST!.” He repeated it over and over in his head. “Eat a good breakfast, get lots of rest, don’t be tardy, DO YOUR BEST”.

Page 4

Earlier that morning on the bus Johnny had shared his little rap with his friend Dylan. Johnny said, “I’m going to ace this test. Listen to how I memorized everything.” Dylan smiled, “Great Johnny, but you know that this test isn’t going to ask about that kind of thing. Those were important things to do to get ready for the test.”

“What?” said Johnny. “Don’t get mad because I studied for this test. I memorized what Mrs. Prince taught us. Didn’t you? This test is a big deal, Dylan!! Don’t say I didn’t tell you so.” Dylan tried to talk to his friend, but Johnny was in his know-it-all mood. The boys walked into the building, hurried to their classroom and got ready for the test.

Page 5

Activity 5.2

KNOW IT ALL

STORY CONNECTION

Now Johnny was sitting in his desk. He smiled and looked down at his test booklet on his desk. Mr. Smart said, "You may now open your test booklet and begin." Johnny was ready for all the questions about test preparation. Johnny stared at the questions. Gulp! He read the first question "In this sentence which word should be capitalized?" The next question said, "Look at the paragraph above and mark which one is the topic sentence." Johnny was confused. This was language arts. And next was a math section, and then a reading section! Johnny thought that Mrs. Prince had taught them everything they would need to know for this test. He certainly didn't know it all this time!!! He looked up at Dylan who had a smile on his face. He knew exactly what Dylan would say on the bus ride home. "Told you so." And he did too.

Page 6

Back Cover

Activity 5.2

TEST TAKING BINGO

Directions: Use these phrases to create your own bingo card.

Eat a good breakfast	**Bubble in whole circle**	**Stay Calm**
Be on time to school	**Eyes on your own test**	**Get lots of rest.**
Use a number 2 pencil	**Erase any stray marks**	**Do your Best**
Double check your answers	**Work Quietly**	**Free Space**

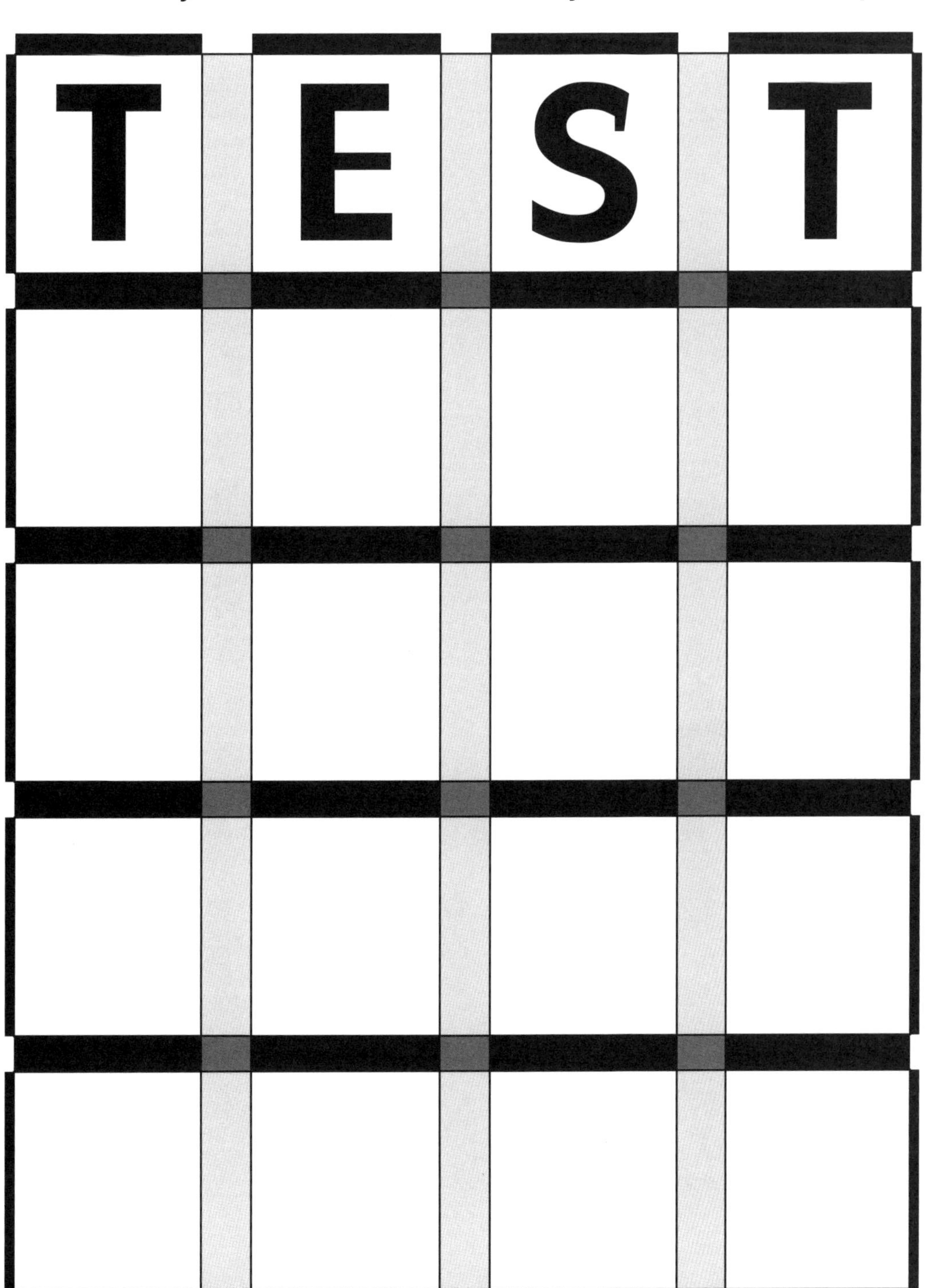

Activity 5.3

TEST TAKING PUZZLES CENTERS

Overview: Students will complete different puzzles about test taking to review appropriate test taking skills.

ASCA Indicator:
A:A1.5 Identify attitudes and behaviors, which lead to successful learning

Materials: Word Scramble page 127, Word Search page 129, Crossword Puzzle page 128,

Procedures:

1.Set up for areas in a classroom for different centers having to do with testing.

2.There are two ways to run centers. First, you could allow students about 7 minutes in each center and simultaneously change centers. Another option is to allow the students to go around the centers and complete at least 3 out of the 4 centers available.

3. After the time to complete centers is up, discuss the following questions:

- Did you stress out when a friend next to you was done first?
- Did you stress when the teacher walked behind you?
- Did you keep your eyes your own paper?
- Did you get confused on any of the puzzles at first?
- How did you feel when the teacher said you have a few minutes left?
- Did anyone make noises that disturbed you?

Worksheet 5.3A

WORD SCRAMBLE

Name: ______________________________

Directions: Unscramble the words below:

hneW ___ ___ ___ ___

ouy ___ ___ ___

ntod' ___ ___ ___ ___

uddrsaentn ___ ___ ___ ___ ___ ___ ___ ___ ___ ___

seusqotin ___ ___ ___ ___ ___ ___ ___ ___ ___

no ___ ___

hte ___ ___ ___

sett ___ ___ ___ ___

tyr ___ ___ ___

ruoy ___ ___ ___ ___

tsbe ___ ___ ___ ___

Write out the sentence with the words from above:

___ ___ ___ ___ ___ ___ ___ ___ ___ ___ ___

___ ___ ___ ___ ___ ___ ___ ___ ___ ___

___ ___ ___ ___ ___ ___ ___ ___ ___ ___ ___ ___ ___ ___

___ ___ ___ ___ ___ ___ ___ ___ ___ ___ ___ ___ ___ ___ ___.

Worksheet 5.3B

CROSSWORD
TESTING SKILLS

Name: ____________________

Across

1. On the test, you need to do your ______.
3. When answering a question on the test, you need to fill in the entire ______.
4. You will need to use a number two ______ for the test.
6. On the test, you should erase all ______ marks.
7. You need to go to bed on time to make sure you get lots of ______.

Down

1. The most important meal on the morning of the test.
2. It is very important to be on ______ to school.
5. The nervous feeling that you get before a big test.

Worksheet 5.3C

Name: ______________________________

BREAKFAST	BUBBLE
ERASE	CONCENTRATE
EXAM	GUESS
PENCIL	QUIZ
REST	STRESS
STUDY	TIME

This is a Test Word Search

N	B	Z	N	Q	E	E	T	B	D	E	W	F	I	O
G	U	P	X	U	V	S	X	T	T	I	D	E	V	A
Q	B	S	B	I	D	J	A	A	A	B	C	A	T	Y
H	B	S	Z	Z	M	G	R	R	M	K	B	J	Q	G
O	L	E	W	C	C	T	N	S	E	W	I	R	Z	W
P	E	U	C	H	N	B	R	E	A	K	F	A	S	T
S	E	G	K	E	P	T	Q	L	B	G	F	J	R	J
W	I	N	C	A	S	Z	N	K	E	U	Q	O	M	S
M	P	N	C	E	W	S	T	I	M	E	F	G	L	Y
J	O	S	R	I	T	L	X	U	W	F	G	Y	Y	N
C	A	X	T	R	L	N	X	E	C	Z	R	X	U	M
S	N	N	E	C	Q	O	Y	G	J	K	V	W	X	P
T	N	S	W	H	D	G	Z	D	K	H	V	C	I	J
B	S	Y	D	U	T	S	Z	Y	X	S	R	I	X	R
E	V	M	Q	H	R	O	C	J	K	N	R	G	D	R

Activity 5.4

1, 2, 3 ACTION ROLE PLAYS

WHAT TO DO (AND WHAT NOT TO DO) ON A TEST

Overview: Students will act out situations where following through with responsibilities leads to natural consequences.

ASCA Indicator:
C:A2.8 Understand the importance of responsibility, dependability, punctuality, integrity and effort in the workplace

Materials: Role-play cards (pg 131)

Procedures:

1. Introduce the lesson by discussing the importance of active listening
2. Split the class into office groups (see explanation of office group pg 12)
3. Distribute a role-play card to each group. (Copy the role play cards on page 131) and assign a director in each group.
4. Explain to class that we will be in our office groups for only 10 minutes and the skits should be no more than one minute.
5. The Director's role is to oversee decision-making and helping to direct the skit. A good director isn't bossy, but is there to oversee and help make decisions if there is an argument.
6. The group should practice and all students in the group should sit with their heads down when they are ready to let the facilitator know the group is ready.
7. To begin the skit the facilitator explains that to start the skits we will act like Hollywood and we will count to three, clap in unison and says action to begin each skit.
8. Practice "1,2,3 Action"
9. The Director from the first office group introduces their group and the counselor leads the class in saying 1,2,3 Action to signal the group to perform. Subsequently, other groups perform.
10. After the skits, the facilitator leads a discussion asking these questions:
    a. What are some important ways to prepare for tests?
    b. What are some behaviors that others might do to disturb you during a test?
    c. How can you make sure to do your best on a test?
    d. What are some ways to calm down if you get nervous on a test?

Activity 5.4

ROLE PLAY CARDS

WHAT TO DO (AND WHAT NOT TO DO) ON A TEST

Small groups of students can practice these role-plays and then perform in front of the class to illustrate the importance of test taking skills.

EATING HABITS BEFORE A TEST

Testing Role Play Card #1

IF YOU FEEL REALLY SICK DURING TEST TIME

Testing Role Play Card #2

WHAT TIME TO GO TO BED BEFORE A TEST

Testing Role Play Card #3

WHAT TO DO WHEN YOU ARE FINISHED WITH THE TEST

Testing Role Play Card #4

WHEN TO GET TO SCHOOL ON THE DAY OF A TEST

Testing Role Play Card #5

WHAT TO DO IF YOU GET NERVOUS ON A TEST

Testing Role Play Card #6

BUBBLING IN ANSWERS ON A TEST

Testing Role Play Card #7

KEEPING YOUR EYES ON YOUR OWN PAPER DURING A TEST

Testing Role Play Card #8

Activity 5.5

LITERATURE LINK:
TESTING MS. MALARKEY

Overview: Through this literature link, students will enjoy a story and write their own class book illustrating the test readiness ideas discussed in the book.

ASCA Indicator:
A:A1.5 Identify attitudes and behaviors, which lead to successful learning

Materials: *Testing Miss Malarkey* by Judy Finchler, pages printed for the class book, title page of class book saying *Testing Ms. __________'s Class.*

Procedures:

1. Discuss the upcoming testing. Who is excited? Who likes testing? Who really hates testing time? Regardless of how you feel about testing, it's important to remember to try your best and to understand some important things about test preparation.
2. Read *Testing Miss Malarkey* by Judy Finchler.
3. Say, "This is a pretty silly book that tells some important lessons on testing, but I think we can write a better book about Testing Ms. __________'s Class. (Have the title page ready with their class name).
4. Present the blank pages that will go in the class book. Tell the students that they will work with a partner to illustrate a page for the class book. The topic they will illustrate can be written on top of each page. A sample page is enclosed. Ideas for page topics are:
   - We've talked a lot about testing.
   - We learned when the test is happening.
   - We learned that we shouldn't stress about the test.
   - Here are smart foods to eat before testing.
   - I need to go to bed on time during testing.
   - I need to come to school on time.
   - I need to sit quietly when I am done.
   - The circles need to be bubbled in correctly.
   - The test will be timed!
   - Our parents and teachers want us to really concentrate on the test.
   - We need to do our best on the test!
   - And we'll be very glad when it's over!

Worksheet 5.5

SAMPLE PAGE
FOR TESTING MS. ________'S CLASS BOOK

Here are smart foods to eat before testing.

Illustrated by

____

&

____

Chapter 5

Activity 5.6

WHAT DOES YOUR STUDY SPACE LOOK LIKE?

Overview: Encourage students to monitor the importance of a clean study area at home and at school.

ASCA Indicator:
A:A1.5: Identify attitudes and behaviors, which lead to successful learning

A:B2.6 Understand the relationship between classroom performance and success in school

Materials: Desk check (page 134), Worksheet page 135

Procedures:

1. Ask students where they study at home. Ask students to close their eyes and picture where they study. What part of the house is it? Is it the same place everyday for homework and studying?
2. Have students turn to a neighbor and talk about if they think their home study space needs improvement. Does it have enough lighting? Are there distractions around like TV or little brothers? What about at school? How could their desks at school improve organization?
3. Distribute worksheet 5.6. Have the students choose the study space that needs the most improvement. Have them draw a before and after look at organization.
4. Discuss these questions:
   - When doing homework or studying for a test, what does a good study space look like?
   - What are some distractions you have at home when studying?
   - At school, why is it important to keep your desk organized?
   - What are some ways to help stay organized at school?
5. Tell the class that in the next week you will be doing desk checks to see who is keeping their study space organized. (see desk check below)

Worksheet 5.6

Name: ______________________

This is what my study space looks like when it is unorganized:

This is what an organized study space should look like:

Activity 5.7

TESTING TRUE OR FALSE:
SHOW ME THE ANSWER

Overview: Students will test themselves about the facts and myths about test taking skills.

ASCA Indicator:
A:A1.5: Identify attitudes and behaviors, which lead to successful learning

A:B2.6 Understand the relationship between classroom performance and success in school

Materials: 25 copies of True signs laminated, 25 copies of False signs laminated, the true/false questions (page 137)

Procedures:

1. Begin the lesson by playing hangman using the phrase TEST PREPARATION.
2. Ask the students to follow these directions. Remind them that there are no correct answers for this activity, only honest answers.
   - Stand up if you get nervous before a test.
   - Stand up if you love taking tests. (Discuss how you can feel both at the same time)
   - Stand up if your bedtime is the earlier on test night than on other nights.
   - Stand up if you feel like you know all the rules about test preparation.
3. Tell the class, "Everyone could use a review and we will see how many of you really know the facts about test preparation skills. Now we'll play a game to see how much you know."
4. Explain to class that when standardized testing begins, they will have to be patient and quiet while the teacher is distributing the materials as they should be practicing now.
5. Distribute one True sign and one False sign to each student face down on the desk.
6. Tell the students the directions for the game, "Keep your signs on your desk face down. Listen to the statement I read and when I say, "Show me the Answer" show me the appropriate sign (if you think the statement is true hold up true sign facing me, or the false sign if you think it is false. Do not show your answer until I say 'Show me the answer.' If you get it right you get a point. Please keep track of your own points, although points really don't matter."
7. Read the statement on the Testing True or False: Show me the Answer Statements on page 137 giving the answer after everyone has shown you their answer.
8. Discuss the following questions:
   - Were any of you tempted to look at someone else's answer? (Remember on a test you really can't do that!)
   - What are some skills you were reminded of today that will help you get ready for testing?

Activity 5.7

TESTING TRUE OR FALSE...

SHOW ME THE ANSWER STATEMENTS!!

Example:

The morning before a test, you should eat a good healthy breakfast.

(True, food is fuel for the brain)

1. **On the night before the big standardized test, you need to study.** *(False, you should try your best on these tests, but there is nothing to study for specifically.)*
2. **You need to be at school before the test begins, but it is fine if you are a little late to school the morning of the test.** *(False, you should start your day with the normal routine so that you do not feel pressured on the day of the test. It is always important to be on time to school.)*
3. **When you are done with the test you can talk quietly to your neighbor if they are also done with the test.** *(False, you must sit silently until your teacher gives you further instructions.)*
4. **You need to make sure to get six to eight hours of sleep on the night of a test.** *(False, you should go to bed at your normal bedtime or a little earlier. Nine or more hours of sleep is considered a healthy night sleep for a student your age.)*

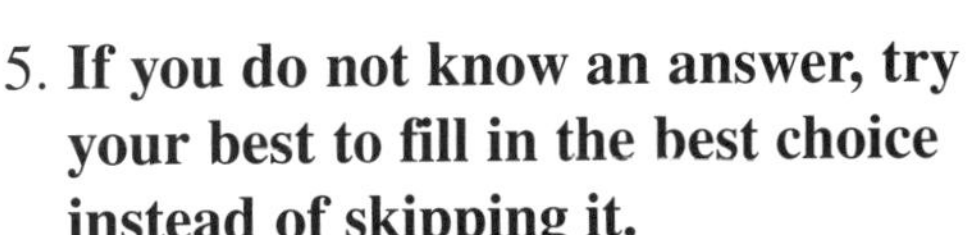

5. **If you do not know an answer, try your best to fill in the best choice instead of skipping it.** *(True, on the test it is beneficial to take your best guess. This way you have a chance of getting the answer correct.)*
6. **When working on the test, you should work as quickly as possible.** *(False, you should go at medium speed.)*
7. **You should erase all of the stray marks and only mark in the bubbles on the answer sheet.** *(True)*
8. **If all you have is a pen, you may use it as long as it has black ink.** *(False, you can only use a number 2 pencil.)*
9. **If you get anxious or nervous on tests, then you might not do well on the test.** *(False, everyone gets a little anxious on tests)*
10. **If you get confused on the test, ask your teacher, and he/she will help you to understand the problem.** *(False, on a standardized test, the teacher can only say, "Just try your best.")*

Signs 5.7A and 5.7B

TRUE

FALSE

Activity 5.8

TESTING MAGIC SQUARE

Overview: Students will examine test readiness skills through creating a hands-on game.

ASCA Indicator:
A:A1.5 Identify attitudes and behaviors, which lead to successful learning

Materials: Magic Square Worksheet page 140

Procedures:

1. Review test taking skills that the students have learned in years passed.
2. Distribute the test taking magic square on page 140.
3. Have students follow the directions and create their magic square. Allow students to pair up with a partner.
4. Tell students, "With your partner follow these directions with one person using their magic square first and the other one gets to be the "chooser." When you are using your magic square tell the chooser to:
   - Pick a number (then you count out that number and open and close the magic square for each number counted).
   - Then ask the chooser, " What feeling do you get about taking tests?"
   - Then uncover that flap with that feeling and ask the chooser the question written there.
5. When each person in the pair has been the chooser you can have the class switch partners and repeat this activity.

Worksheet 5.8

TESTING MAGIC SQUARE

Directions for how to make your testing magic square:

1. Cut along the solid lines of the outer square.
2. With the writing facing down, fold each corner to the center.
3. Then, turn the paper over and fold the corners to the center again.
4. Fold the paper in half with the circle facing the outside.
5. Write different numbers of your choice (1-10) in each circle.
6. With both hands, put your pointer and thumb under the paper flaps. The numbers within the circles are showing on the top.

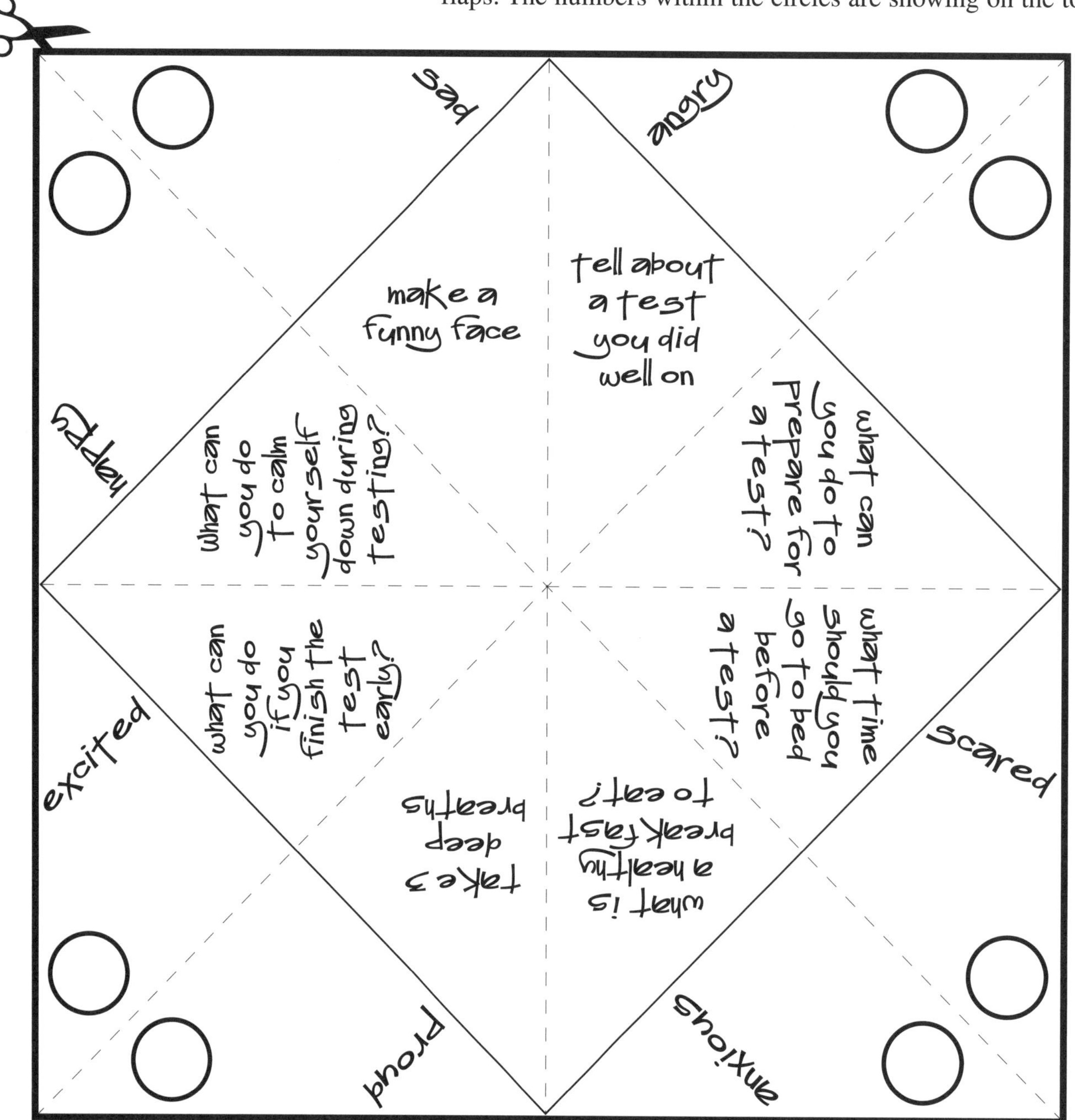

Chapter 6

LEARNING STYLES

****This chapter is appropriate for the latter part of third grade through fifth grade.*

Students are constantly being talked to about their learning, but rarely do they think about how they learn. It is important to give students insight into the different ways that they learn. Once they can identify their strength, they can develop better ways to study and have a better understanding of how they can attain knowledge. Within this chapter, you will find child-friendly lessons and activities to teach students about the different styles with which they learn.

Indicators from ASCA National Model that are addressed in this chapter (see crosswalk pg 21):

A:A1.5 ....Identify Attitudes and behaviors which lead to successful learning

A:A2.4 ....Apply knowledge and learning styles to positively influence school performance

A:B2.6......Understand the relationship between classroom performance and success in school.

C:A1.4......Learn how to interact and work cooperatively in teams

Chapter Contents

PRE-POST SURVEY
FOR LEARNING STYLES

Overview: To assess student perception of different learning styles.

ASCA Indicator:
A:A1.5: Identify attitudes and behaviors which lead to successful learning.

Materials Needed:
Learning Styles Survey

Procedures:

1. Distribute Learning Styles Survey before the lesson(s) you intend to do on learning styles.
2. Compile the results to give you an idea of how the group/class feels about learning styles.
3. Repeat the survey at the end of the lesson(s) to assess what the students have learned.

Learning Styles Student Survey

	Strongly Agree	Agree	Disagree	Strongly Disagree
I can recognize three learning styles.	❑	❑	❑	❑
I can identify what learning style best describes me.	❑	❑	❑	❑
I understand that all of the students in my class have different learning styles.	❑	❑	❑	❑
I know studying strategies for each learning style.	❑	❑	❑	❑

Learning how to learn is life's most important skill.

— Tony Buzan

Date:

Dear Parent/Guardian,

Students are constantly surrounded by the concept of learning, but rarely do they think about how they learn. It is important to give students insight into the different ways that they learn. Those students who have strong listening skills might learn to study in different ways than students who have a higher level of visual learning. In our guidance lesson, we will be discussing three types of learning styles visual (learning by seeing), auditory (learning by listening), and kinesthetic (learning by experiencing or movement). Once they can identify their learning strengths, they can develop better ways to study and have a better understanding of how they can attain knowledge. This would be a great opportunity for you to discuss your strengths, weaknesses and learning style with your child. Thank you for helping your child understand more about ways to be successful in the lifelong learning process.

Sincerely,

School Counselor

Activity 6.1

POETRY LINK

I'M ALWAYS LATE

Overview: Students will discover different learning styles through this activity with hands on activity.

ASCA Indicators:
A:A2.4 Apply knowledge and learning styles to positively influence school performance

Materials: Poem, baking supplies (rice cakes, peanut butter, cream cheese, M&M's®, raisins, licorice), written directions, bag of mini rice cakes or candy as treat (make label and tape on bag saying "Learning Style Munchies")

Procedures:

1. Read the poem on page 145 to the class.
2. Tell the class that you will need three volunteers to demonstrate the three learning styles.
3. Have the three volunteers go out of the classroom door so that they cannot see or hear what is being done.
4. Explain to the class that you will be teaching each student how to make a rice cake funny face using some of these directions. Tell the class, "As I am teaching these students with the different learning styles, imagine which one would be difficult for you. Which would be easy?" (Optional for classroom management: Tell students that you will share some of this candy with them, but only if they are an appropriate audience.)
5. Using various ingredients (listed above in materials), make a smiley face using these different learning techniques.
   a. ***Visual Learning Technique:*** Show directions to make the funny face.
   b. ***Auditory Learning Technique:*** Tell them the directions without showing them.
   c. ***Kinesthetic Learning Technique:*** Have students do the creating of "rice cake funny face."
6. Discuss the following questions
   - Do you think you could combine these learning styles?
   - Which was easiest for you?
   - What style do you think teachers usually use to teach?

LEARNING WITH OUR SENSES

BY JOAN KING

From the day that we are born, there are a ton of things to learn.
So much to know, so much to do, new things at every turn.
We HEAR the sounds that make up words before we start to read,
And then we SEE the alphabet before we can succeed.

We PLAY a lot of games with words, with singing, painting, dancing
Because such different ways to learn can only be enhancing!
When Mom first taught me how to bake, she READ OUT LOUD to me.
She then set out ingredients so I could look and SEE.

She showed me just what I should DO and then I DID the same,
And so my learning how to bake was like a little game!
Each one of us learns differently, let's not put on pretenses,
But we can all have more success if we learn with ALL OUR SENSES!

Activity 6.2

STORY CONNECTION

DIFFERENT WAYS TO LEARN

Overview: Students will hear descriptions of the different learning styles.

ASCA Indicator:
A:A2.4 Apply knowledge and learning styles to positively influence school performance

Materials: Copy of story (pages 147), drawing paper, markers/crayons

Procedures:

1. Read story to the class.
2. Divide class into groups of two.
3. Have each group decide on a character from the story to illustrate. If they would like to create another name for another relative of this family (ie- Kinesthetic Kyle, Visual Vickie, etc.)
4. After every pair has finished this task, have them introduce their character to the class.
5. Discuss how many people chose a certain learning style.

Activity 6.2

DIFFERENT WAYS TO LEARN

STORY CONNECTION

Koby loved when the counselor, Ms. Nguyen came to his class to do a guidance lesson. Every so often, his class went to the counselor's center room and Koby loved that too. The students would go to each center and learn about different things. Usually in guidance lessons, Ms. Nguyen would teach them about how to get along and how to solve problems. Recently Ms. Nguyen taught about learning styles, which for Koby was a new thing to think about. Ms. Nguyen told the class about how everyone learns in a different way. She talked about auditory learning, visual learning, and kinesthetic learning and all the students discovered how they learned best. It was slightly confusing for Koby because he just thought everyone learned with his or her brains. He didn't really think about the different part of your brain that does the learning.

That night he had a very bizarre dream. In his dream things at his house were bubbling with energy. Everyone was moving and seemed to be busy. His sister Lori was listening to a new CD. His sister Connie was creating a model of the planets for a science project, and his sister Shelby was watching

a TV show on oceanography. The dream would not have been so bizarre, except for what his sisters were wearing. Lori was wearing a shirt that said *Listening Lori*. Connie had on a shirt that said *Creating Connie*, and Shelby had on a baseball hat that said *See it Shelby*.

In his dream, Koby was walking around his house and his sisters were constantly doing activities but they were only doing activities that applied to the learning style they were representing. Lori was listening to the radio, listening to the birds, even listening to a tape of her own voice repeating her spelling words. Connie was moving around acting out her social studies chapter. She was pretending she was President Lincoln giving his grand speech: "Four score and seven years ago." When Connie studied for her spelling test she drew out the words in chocolate icing. Shelby was acting strange too. She was watching a video on how to be a better tennis player. When she studied for her health quiz, she read her textbook and closed her eyes and kept saying, "Visualize the page."

Koby woke up startled. He came downstairs from his bedroom for breakfast and sat with his sisters. He rubbed his eyes and knew that his dream must have been because of Ms. Nguyen's lesson on learning styles. He tried to tell his youngest sister about his dream, but this time Lori wasn't listening.

Activity 6.3

WORD SEARCH

CAN YOU FIND YOUR LEARNING STYLE?

Name: ______________________

AUDITORY	DOING
EXPLORE	KINESTHETIC
LEARN	PRACTICE
STUDY	STYLE
UNDERSTAND	VISUAL

C E M U Q L Y Y E V N W J E V
P I F D B J R D Q X S V R L I
D K T T I O Y N V B P W K Y S
R E Z E T N R A E L C L Q T U
D M M I H C J T I N O L O S A
X U D X E T R S T J D A E R L
B U I E B R S R V S M N F B E
A Z O V J Z Z E J M R X V L X
H Y T W O C J D N W Y X N D G
R J D I P R J N K I B J O G H
C F A U D N P U H J K I W Q E
P R A C T I C E B A N P J I X
K V R T H S H I F G Y F Y E S
E J I E C Z N U D U V Y L L I
L O S T P U B U K W P F I X E

Activity 6.4

MAKE A BOOKMARK WITH YOUR LEARNING STYLE

Directions:

Create a bookmark of your learning style.

Are you a visual, auditory or kinesthetic learner?

When you are done decorating, tie some yarn in the hole on the top.

Activity 6.5

LEARNING STYLE SECRET MESSAGE

Overview: Through this game, students will learn about learning styles.

ASCA Indicator:
A:A2.4 Apply knowledge and learning styles to positively influence school performance

Materials: Worksheet 6.5.1, Worksheet 6.5.2 , Signs 6.5A, Sign 6.5B, Sign 6.5C , a treat

Procedures:

1. Read Poem from page 145.

2. Tell class that you will be explaining to them three different styles of learning.

   (If you taught a learning-style lesson last year, see if students can recall the three learning styles)

3. Explain what the three types are in the following way

   a. For the visual learning style, hold up Sign 6.5A.

   b. Tell them what auditory learning is so that they are learning this by listening.

   c. Have them stand up and make the letter K with their bodies and say "Kinesthetic means moving"

4. Distribute Activity 6.5 worksheet. Have them turn to the side of the grid and follow these directions with the three learning styles.

   - Point to block 1A (show them how to find the box using the columns and rows). Without pointing say, "In block 1A write the letter W. In block 1B write the letter E." (This is using auditory learning).

   - On your copy of the grid, draw a smiley face in block 6E. Walk around the class with it and say, "Do this." (This is using visual learning).

   - In row 6 write the word "differently" anywhere in that row. (Ask, "What learning style is being used here?)"

   - Ask students to DO this, "Put your finger on box 1D and draw an imaginary line down to 3D. Now make the line with your pencil. Put your finger on box 1E and draw an imaginary line down to 3E. Now make the line with your pencil." (this is kinesthetic learning—doing it first)

   - Write the word "Learn" on the board. Tell class, "Put this word learn in box 4C as small as you can."

5. Ask students if anyone can figure out the secret message, which is 4 words. The message is "We all learn differently." (The "a" in all is missing)

6. Give a treat to the person who figures out the message.

7. Have students turn their paper over and write down one fact about each learning style that they learned.

Worksheet 6.5A

LEARNING STYLE SECRET MESSAGE

Name: ______________________________

Directions: Follow the directions your counselor gives you to find the secret message.

What is the secret message?

__ __ __ __ __ __ __ __ __ __ __

__ __ __ __ __ __ __ __ __ __ __

	A	B	C	D	E
1					
2					
3					
4					
5					
6					

LEARNING STYLE SECRET MESSAGE

What is the secret message?

W E A L L L E A R N
D I F F E R E N T L Y

	A	B	C	D	E
1	W	E			
2			a (is missing)		
3					
4			learn		
5					
6	Dif	fer	en	tly	

Worksheet 6.5B

HOW ARE YOU SMART?

Name: ______________________________

Directions: While your counselor explains about each type of learning please take notes about what you are learning.

Auditory

____

____

____

Kinesthetic

____

____

____

Visual

____

____

____

Sign 6.5A

AUDITORY LEARNING

Listen to your counselor tell you about auditory learning.

Sign 6.5B

VISUAL LEARNING

Typically, you will remember 40% of what you see.

Visual Learners can remember better from using charts, diagrams, videos, and written directions.

Visual learners remember things by making to-do lists and writing in their assignment books.

Sign 6.5C

KINESTHETIC LEARNING (MOVEMENT)

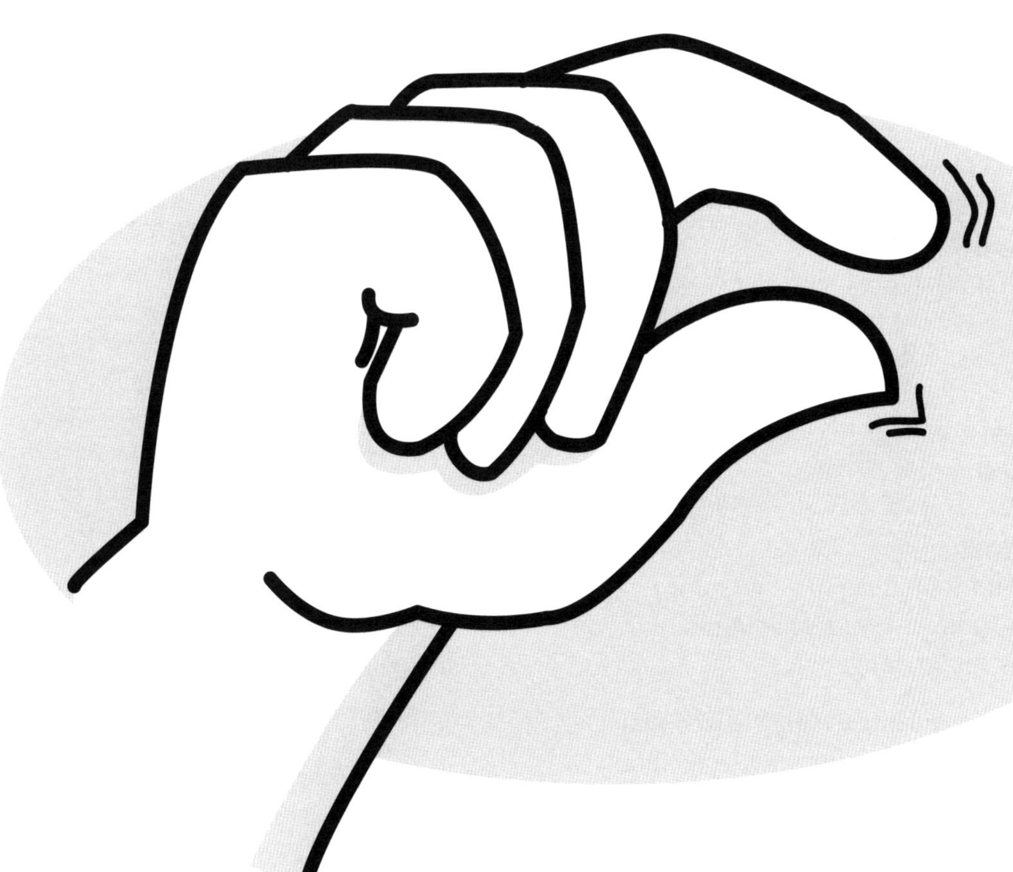

Make up a movement to help you remember this word.

Activity 6.6

LEARNING STYLES CENTERS

Overview: Students explore multi-sensory centers about leaning styles.

ASCA Indicator:
A:A2.4 Apply knowledge and learning styles to positively influence school performance

Materials: Worksheet 6.6A, Worksheet 6.6B

Procedures:

1. Set up four areas in a classroom for different centers having to do with learning styles.
2. Divide students evenly between the centers set up. Allow students about 7 minutes in each center and simultaneously change centers at the sound of a bell. Another option is to allow the students to go around to the 3 centers of their choice and in the time allotted, completing at least 3 out of the 4 centers available.
3. Here are some examples of centers that can be set up:
   - ***Word Search Center***
     Materials: Worksheet 6.3, pencils
   - ***Listening Center***
     Materials: listening center with cassette player attached to headphones, a tape made giving directions of words to spell and math problems to do, or an audio book.
   - ***Identify Your Learning Style Center***
     Materials: Worksheet 6.6A, pencils
   - ***Silent Reading Center***
     Materials: books checked out from your school library (or in your personal library) that have significance to learning style, the brain, study skills, etc.
   - ***Graphing Center***
     Materials: Worksheet 6.6B, crayons/markers

Worksheet 6.6A

LEARNING STYLES INVENTORY

Name: ______________________

Date: ______________________

Directions:
1). Fold the paper lengthwise down the dotted line. Check the boxes beside the sentences that describe you.

		auditory	visual	kinesthetic
1.	❑ I remember something better if I write it down.		x	
2.	❑ I need to take a lot of study breaks.			x
3.	❑ Writing is difficult for me.	x		
4.	❑ If there is music or noise around, I can't concentrate.		x	
5.	❑ I learn well by using math cubes, counters and acting things out.			x
6.	❑ I like to hear directions told to me rather than reading them.	x		
7.	❑ I hum or talk to myself when I am bored.	x		
8.	❑ To remember something better, I get a picture of it in my head.		x	
9.	❑ I use my hands when I am talking.			x
10.	❑ I learn well by reading things out loud.	x		
11.	❑ I like to see what I am learning better than hearing it explained.		x	
12.	❑ I like to do things myself to really understand things.			x
	TOTALS			

2). Unfold the paper and circle the x on the same line of your check marks.

3). Next, add up the number of circled x's in each column and mark the totals.

What type of learner are you?

❑ auditory ❑ visual ❑ kinesthetic

Chapter 6

Worksheet 6.6B

GRAPH OF LEARNING STYLES IN THIS CLASS

LOOK AT OUR LEARNING STYLES

Group Name: ______________________

Group Members Names: ______________________

____

____

____

____

Directions: Make a graph of what types of learners are in your group.

Auditory	**Kinesthetic**	**Visual**

Chapter 7

ACTIVE LISTENING SKILLS

Listening skills are important in all aspects of communication. Students are implored to listen to parents, teachers and friends. Sometimes they need to build their skills set in knowing better ways to actively listen. This chapter gives students ideas of how to better pay attention and show an active listening stance. Professional students need to understand not only better ways to listen, but also the consequences of not paying attention.

Chapter 7

Indicators from ASCA National Model that are addressed in this chapter (see crosswalk pg 21):

A:A1.2 ....Display a positive interest in learning.

A:A1.5 ....Identify Attitudes and behaviors which lead to successful learning

A:B2.6......Understand the relationship between classroom performance and success in school.

C.C2.3 ......Learn to work cooperatively with others as a team member

PS-A1.8....Understand the need for self-control and how to practice it

PS-A2.7....Know that communication involves speaking, listening and nonverbal behavior.

Chapter Contents

PRE-POST SURVEY
FOR LISTENING SKILLS

Overview: To assess student perception on active listening.

ASCA Indicator:
A:A1.5: Identify attitudes and behaviors which lead to successful learning.

Materials Needed:
Listening Survey

Procedures:

1. Distribute Listening Survey before the lesson(s) you intend to do on time management.
2. Compile the results to give you an idea of how the group/class feels about time management and what their perceptions are.
3. Repeat the survey at the end of the lesson(s) to assess what the students have improved on and how perceptions have changed.

Student Survey on Listening Skills

	Strongly Agree	Agree	Disagree	Strongly Disagree
I am a good listener.	❑	❑	❑	❑
I look at the person when he/she is talking.	❑	❑	❑	❑
I think good listening skills are important.	❑	❑	❑	❑
I should lean forward a little when I am listening.	❑	❑	❑	❑
Good listeners usually have more friends.	❑	❑	❑	❑
I notice how others feel when I don't listen.	❑	❑	❑	❑
I need to improve my active listening skills.	❑	❑	❑	❑

Nature gave us one tongue and two ears so we could hear twice as much as we speak.

— Epictetus

Date:

Dear Parent/Guardian,

One skill that has great importance at school and at home is the skill of listening. Clearly, you as a parent would love to have your child listen to you the first time you give them a direction. Equally, teachers at school would love for children to have a greater aptitude in listening to directions, listening for learning, and listening to others in order to get along. In our guidance lessons we will be practicing skills for good listening and the importance of paying attention. The certain physical skills we will be teaching for active listening are: eye contact, nodding your head, and acting interested in what someone is saying. This would be a great time for your family to discuss how listening skills are important both at home and at school. Make sure to ask your child what he/she has learned. Thank you for helping your child understand the link between important life skills and school success.

Sincerely,

School Counselor

Activity 7.1

POETRY LINK
CONCENTRATE

Overview: Create "Listen and Concentrate book" by using this poem as the text.

ASCA Indicators:
C.C2.3 Learn to work cooperatively with others as a team member

PS-A1.8 Understand the need for self-control and how to practice it

Materials: Poem (page 165), drawing paper on which one line of this poem on page 165 is written on the top.

Procedures:

1. Read the poem to the class and review listening skills (you can refer to the poster on page 174 N'CLASS) to teach these skills.
2. Discussion Questions:
   a. What are some things that make your mind wander?
   b. What are some times when adults expect kids to listen?
   c. What are some times when it is hard to listen?
   d. What are some good listening skills mentioned in this poem?
   e. How does paying attention lead to more play time?
3. After discussing the poem and the above question, hand out one page of the drawing paper poem to each student.
4. Students can work alone or with a partner (depending on how many kids are in the group) to illustrate the line of the poem that they have received.
5. Compile the pages and bind them as a book. Use the full poem as the first page.

CONCENTRATION

BY JOAN KING

When I am told a thing to do

Like make my bed or tie my shoe,

My brain takes off and starts to wander

And dream of things of which I'm fonder.

Like TV shows or favorite books,

Like playing ball or babbling brooks.

I guess that I should CONCENTRATE,

Just do those things that just can't wait.

With eye contact, and nodding head

Not daydreaming of lunch instead,

Sitting up and shoulders square

These tricks sure help me be aware

And if I put my efforts there,

I find I have playtime to spare!

Activity 7.2

STORY CONNECTION

WONDERFUL LISTENING STORY

Overview: Through reading a short story and answering questions, students will understand the importance of active listening skills.

ASCA Indicators:
PS-A1.8 Understand the need for self-control and how to practice it

PS-A2.7 Know that communication involves speaking, listening and nonverbal behavior

Materials: copies of story on pages 167-168

Procedures:

1. Ask if anyone in the class knows why listening is so important. Tell the class we will do an interactive story to understand more about listening.
2. Split class into office groups. Assign each office group a word. Tell them that when they hear the word they must respond with the following sound and motion.

office group 1

hear this:	*do this:*
frustrated—	make "ughh" sound and clench fists

office group 2

hear this:	*do this:*
once—	say "one time" and put one finger in the air

office group 3

hear this:	*do this:*
quiet—	say "hush" and put finger to lips

office group 4

hear this:	*do this:*
wonderful—	say "hooray" with hands in the air

office group 5

hear this:	*do this:*
lion—	say "roar" and act like lion

3. Read story aloud to the class while groups participate with sounds and motions.

Discussion Questions:

- What did Darla learn about listening?
- When are important times to listen?
- How did you know when to make your sound?
- How did you stay alert? Was this easy or hard?
- How could Darla have used active listening techniques to stay alert and listen when her teacher was talking about more boring subjects?

Activity 7.2

WONDERFUL LISTENING STORY

STORY CONNECTION

"What did you say? What page are we on? What did she say? Do we have homework?" Darla always seemed to ask questions. Sometimes they were questions that the teacher had just answered. Her teacher, Mr. Smart got ***frustrated***, because he really wanted his students to listen. He wanted to say his directions only ***once***, but it never failed that someone wasn't listening. Often one of the students who wasn't listening was Darla.

One day Mr. Smart asked that the class get quiet for an important announcement. He told them that the next week they were going on a field trip. Suddenly everyone was listening. "***Wonderful,***" Mr. Smart said. " Now that I have everyone's attention, I'll tell you what you must do in order to go on this field trip. First you must bring back your permission slip. Second, you must be ***quiet*** when I give the rules at the zoo. "The zoo!" the students cheered. "We're going to the zoo?" asked Matthew. "Yes", said Mr. Smart. And I must tell you about the special thing we will see. There is a dangerous ***lion*** they have on exhibit and in order to stay safe, we must follow the rules." Mr. Smart was excited because everyone listened when he said it only ***once***. "***Wonderful***," he said.

On the day of the field trip, many parents accompanied the class to the zoo. Mr. Smart asked all of the students to raise their hand if their parents were coming on the field trip. Darla wasn't listening so she didn't raise her hand, even though her mom was coming. When her mom walked in, Mr. Smart looked ***frustrated*** and his face got red and blotchy. He took a deep breath. When all of the teachers, parents, and students got on the bus, Mr. Smart asked everyone to be ***quiet***. He wanted to say the rules for the zoo just ***once***. He told the students that when they got to the zoo, they needed to stay with their assigned buddy, they should not touch any of the animals, and under no circumstances should they feed the ***lion***. As you know, Mr. Smart liked to only say directions ***once***, but since this was such an important rule, he said it again. "Remember, DO NOT, NOT, NOT feed the lion. Does everyone understand?" They all nodded. "***Wonderful***," he said.

Activity 7.2

WONDERFUL LISTENING STORY

STORY CONNECTION

When the class got to the zoo, they were so excited that they didn't even hear Mr. Smart trying to get their attention. He looked ***frustrated*** until everyone got ***quiet***. Mr. Smart told everyone to be back at the bus at noontime. Darla was dragging her mom and her buddy Natasha off the bus while Mr. Smart was still talking. They saw the reptiles and the birds and the elephants. Darla was excited and also hungry. Darla asked her mom, "Can you buy me and Natasha some peanuts?" Darla's mom said yes and bought them each a bag of peanuts. They kept walking through the zoo. They were getting a little ***frustrated*** because they hadn't yet seen the wildcats, which were the feature exhibit.

Finally, as the clock was getting close to noon, they found the wild cats and they could see from afar the mighty ***lion*** that they had heard so much about. Darla and Natasha ate their peanuts and scooted up to the cage and stared into the eyes of the ***lion***. Natasha finished her peanuts and asked Darla, "Do you want me to take your trash?" But Darla really wasn't finished not to mention that she wasn't listening. She was throwing a peanut up in the air. Natasha asked only ***once*** and turned her back to throw away her bag. When Natasha turned around, she couldn't find Darla anywhere and got ***frustrated***. She looked into the lion's den not believing that Darla could disappear so quickly. As she glanced back at the lion, he licked his chops, gave a little burp and Natasha swore she heard him say "Yum, that was ***wonderful***".

Activity 7.3

WORD SEARCH
PAYING ATTENTION

Overview: This is a great activity to let students experience how external distraction affects the ability to pay attention.

ASCA Indicator:
PS-A1.8 Understand the need for self-control and how to practice it

Materials: Word Search, Worksheet 2.3, radio, TV, telephone

Procedure:

1. Distribute word search to students.
2. Tell the class that you are having a contest to see who is the first to find 8 words. Tell the class to treat this like a test and that they might even get a grade on it.
3. If someone asks for you to repeat how many, tell them from now on you will repeat things only once.
4. Turn the TV on. Stand in the back of the room while the TV is on and say in a normal tone voice where one of the words is.
5. Next, turn on the radio or a CD player. Tell them where another word is.
6. Create another distraction such as pretend to talk on the phone, or have a loud conversation with the teacher or tell a joke to a student.
7. Remind the class that we are still having a contest.
8. When someone has found 8 words, give them a small prize and tell the rest of the class to put down their pencils.
9. Discuss the following questions:
   - What do you think this lesson was about?
   - What made it difficult to concentrate? (introduce the word distractions)
   - What are some distractions kids have at school? at home?
   - Where is a good place at home to study where there are few distractions?

Worksheet 7.3

Name: ______________________________

ATTENTION	DIRECTIONS
EARS	UNDERSTAND
HEAR	LEARN
LISTEN	NODDING
LOOK	QUIET
SHOULDERS	EYES

How many words did you find in the allotted time? ____________________

H N F I D N S O A I S M C N S
L O E C N U R E V E V N O N I
U D R Y A R A A Y O H T O Q R
E D R F T Z E E E J C I L D J
P I N L S H E A R L T C Y D R
O N J Y R O G O L C O C O U N
A G O M E L Q H E O M I P Z V
Z T T L D Z J R L G O A H V I
V X T A N X I I Z C M K I C Q
I Q B E U D S H O U L D E R S
N X R Y N T E I U Q W B W M D
Q X K T E T Z U H N U K O T K
V R L N D H I V V V E N U V M
S E F G Z R X O O D O Q J W E
Q B W Z V Y D T N F B H A N H

Activity 7.4

1, 2, 3 ACTION ROLE PLAYS

Overview: Students will act out situations where punctuality, time management and tardiness lead to natural consequences.

ASCA Indicator:
C.C2.3 Learn to work cooperatively with others as a team member

PS-A1.8 Understand the need for self-control and how to practice it

PS-A2.7 Know that communication involves speaking, listening and nonverbal behavior

Materials: Role-play cards (pg 172)

Procedures:

1. Introduce the lesson by discussing the importance of active listening
2. Split the class into office groups (see explanation of office group pg 12)
3. Assign one Director in each group.
4. Distribute role-play card to each group. (Copy the role play cards on page 172)
5. Explain to class that we will be in our office groups for only 10 minutes and the skits should be no more than one minute. The skits can show what is written on the card (a negative behavior) and then the group can do a skit on how to make that an appropriate behavior.
6. The Director's role is to oversee decision-making and help to direct the skit. A good director isn't bossy, but is there to oversee and help make decisions if there is an argument.
7. The group should practice and all students in the group should sit with their heads down when they are ready to let the facilitator know the group is ready.
8. To begin the skit the facilitator explains that to start the skits we will act like Hollywood and we will count to three, clap in unison and says "action" to begin each skit.
9. The Director from the first office group introduces their group and the counselor leads the class in saying 1,2,3 Action to signal the group to perform. Subsequently, other groups perform.
10. After the skits, the facilitator leads a discussion asking these questions:
    - How do people normally feel when they are not listened to?
    - What are some reasons to listen at school?
    - What are some reasons to listen to friends?
    - What are some reasons that professionals should listen at work?

Activity 7.4

ROLE PLAY CARDS

Small groups of students can practice these role-plays and then perform in front of the class to illustrate the importance of paying attention.

A student is not listening to what page the teacher said the assignment was on. He/she comes in the next day and has done the wrong assignment.

Paying Attention Role Play Card #1

A child not is listening to his/her parent giving a list of chores. He/she has a consequence because they have not paid attention to their responsibilities.

Paying Attention Role Play Card #2

Two friends are spending a day together. They are arguing over what TV show to watch. One friend gives an I-Statement and the other friend does not listen to the I-Statement.

Paying Attention Role Play Card #3

A teacher did not listen to a principal giving directions for a fire drill. The teacher has to have a meeting with his/her boss because of this.

Paying Attention Role Play Card #4

A counselor does not listen accurately to a student's problems. The student gets very frustrated.

Paying Attention Role Play Card #5

A taxi driver did not pay attention to a passenger's directions to a store and drove her/him to the wrong place.

Paying Attention Role Play Card #6

Activity 7.5

LEARNING ACTIVE LISTENING SKILLS 'N' CLASS

Overview: This is a concrete set of skills for students to exhibit active listening.

ASCA Indicators:
PS-A2.7 Know that communication involves speaking, listening and nonverbal behavior

Materials: N' Class Poster (page 174)

Procedures:

1. Introduce lesson: Today's lesson is about something you are doing right now. (Listening) Who thinks this is something you are born knowing how to do? Discuss how you can actually learn to listen in a better way called active listening. This is a way to help us to listen when our brains get the wiggles.

2. Today you will learn what I call listening tricks or "how to listen N' class." They are tricks because sometimes you might not be interested in what is being taught(but you still need to trick yourself into listening and remind yourself what good listening looks like. It's important to listen in class and here is how we do it N' Class (go over 'N' CLASS poster page 174)

3. Use the puppet as a model of good listening. Ask a student to tell the puppet a story about their weekend. The puppet will model both good listening skills and poor listening skills. Ask students to be detectives and tell you how they know he is not listening. Then do the same when he is listening.

4. Review the listening tricks that I have taught you before (go over 'N' CLASS poster)

5. Split kids into **A**'s & **B**'s and have them find a partner that is the opposite (**A**'s find **B**'s)

6. Get one pair to come up and model: **A** will listen first in the wrong way. Then switch and have **B** listen in the correct way.

7. Let the whole class practice. Tell **A**'s they will be listeners first and **B**'s will be the talkers. Then switch who is talker and listener. Ideas of subjects to tell them to talk about are:
   a) your first memory of kindergarten
   b) the best gift you have ever received
   c) what you did last weekend
   d) the best vacation you've ever had or
   e) what is your favorite art project you've done in school.

8. Bring class back together and review discussion questions:

   - Who had a partner who they felt was really listening? How did they show you that they were listening?
   - How did it feel when someone was not listening appropriately?
   - Name three adults that would appreciate good listening skills.
   - What made it difficult to listen?
   - How would good listening skills be helpful as a professional student?

Poster 7.5

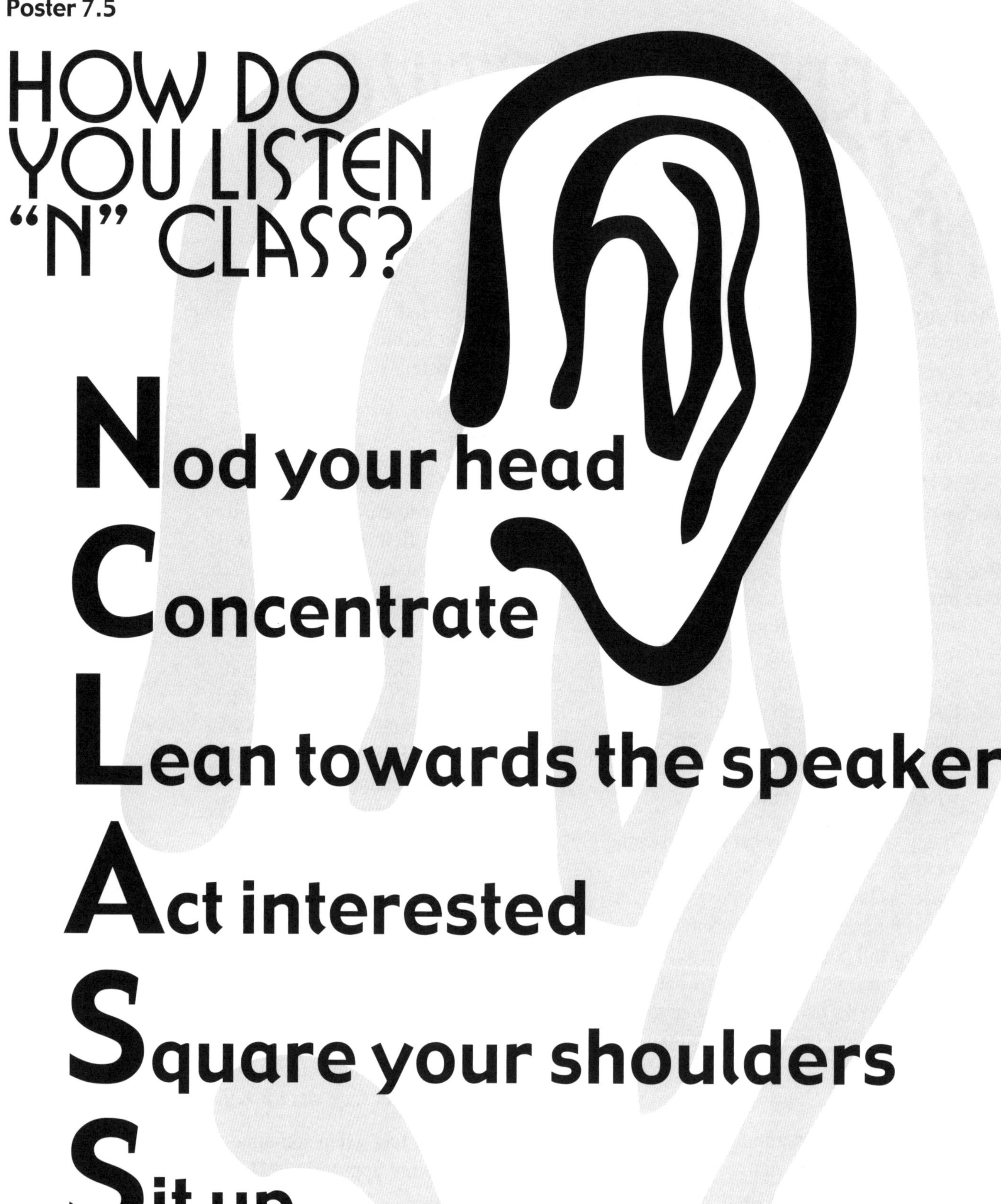
HOW DO YOU LISTEN "N" CLASS?
Nod your head
Concentrate
Lean towards the speaker
Act interested
Square your shoulders
Sit up

Activity 7.6

LISTEN AND FOLLOW DIRECTIONS

AN OLD FAITHFUL SKILL

Overview: This listening game helps students understand the need to pay attention when someone is giving them directions.

ASCA Indicators:
A:A1.5: Identify Attitudes and behaviors which lead to successful learning

Materials: "N" Class Active Listening Poster (page 174), listening game scripts a and b (page 176)

Procedures:

1. Tell class first we will review the listening skills on this poster "N" CLASS (from Activity 7.7). Then we will play a game.
2. Review listening tricks for "N" Class (show poster from page 174)
3. Now, let's play a listening game. Ask for two volunteers. Tell them that they will wait in the hall and be asked to come in one a time. When they come in they will be told the rules of the game. Ask for volunteers who are great listeners and feel like they have good memories too!
4. Have volunteers leave and wait in the hallway. Ask volunteer #1 to come in. Explain the directions to this game. Tell volunteer #1 "This is a listening game. I need someone to go get me some batteries. Will you tell the next person where to go to get them for me? You have to listen and remember so you can tell (next student's name) where to go "
5. Read script* (modify with only 3 lines of the directions for 2nd-3rd grade). Tell the student that you will invite the next student in and they will need to tell that student where to get the batteries, so make sure you remember these directions. Repeat script again up to three times as requested by the student.
6. Invite volunteer #2 into the class and have volunteer #1 tell them the directions from script that they should tell from memory.

* Script A can be used for the younger kids and script B for older ones. Also, you can use both scripts using A for easier and B for more difficult.

7. Point out students who were showing N' Class Skills while the volunteers were speaking in front of the class.

Discussion questions

- Ask volunteers: What was easy or difficult about listening and remembering the directions?
- Was script A or B easier to listen to? Do you listen better (or more) to things like video games or museums and artwork?
- How do you help yourself listen to things that you are unfamiliar or maybe even uninterested in?
- What are situations where listening and remembering directions would be important?

Variation:
Read an explanation of Old Faithful at Yellowstone National Park and bring in Ansel Adams' poster. After explaining, point out who was listening.

Script A

Go to the toy store.

Turn right down aisle number five.

You'll see the video games on your left.

Meet me near the batteries next to the games.

Script B

Let's meet at the museum

Go in the front door

Take a left towards the gift shop

You will see some photographs by Ansel Adams

I'll meet you by the picture of Old Faithful Geyser.

Activity 7.7

PAYING ATTENTION

CALL THE COLOR

Overview: Through this activity, students will experience the importance of concentration and practicing skills.

ASCA Indicator:
A:A1.5 Identify attitudes and behaviors, which lead to successful learning

Materials: Sample of completed Worksheet 7.7 (done on a larger poster board or on an overhead projection), colored markers

Procedures:

1. Ask students to raise their hand if they are good at paying attention.
2. Tell the students to close their eyes and to think about how their classroom looks. Ask them to think about what color the teachers shirt is. See if they were paying attention to other things in the class that have been on the walls all year long.
3. Discuss the importance of paying attention.
4. Show the class the sample of Worksheet 7.7. Ask for a student volunteer to try this exercise of saying the color of the word, not reading the word.
5. Distribute Worksheet 7.7 and allow students to create their own activity,
6. Once the students have completed the worksheet have them pair up with a partner and attempt to read the colors their partner has listed.
7. Have students switch partners and try this again.
8. Get students to go back to their seats and discuss the following questions:
   - What made this difficult?
   - Did this task get easier with practice?
   - What other skills improve with practice?
   - What does concentration have to do with learning?

Variation:
On the Internet go to this website where the Stroop Effect test flashes on the screen. (http://www.colourtherapyhealing.com/colour_fun/stroop_effect_flash.php)

NOTE: websites may change

**This lesson is based upon activities on the Stroop Effect found online.*

Worksheet 7.7

PAYING ATTENTION
CALL THE COLOR

Directions: Color inside the letters with a crayon that is not the same color as what the letters spell. Have a partner tell you the color of the word without reading the word.

Why is it so hard?
You read everyday, so your brain is used to using the skill of reading. When we ask the brain to call the color instead of reading the word, we are sending the brain mixed messages. Our brain is tempted to use the reading skills over the much less practiced skill of saying the color. With practice you will get better at this activity. This shows how with practice we can learn new things!

Concentration is a BIG part of learning!

red

white

brown

black

orange

yellow

blue

Chapter 8

CAREER AWARENESS

Children often start thinking about what they want to do when they grow up at a very young age. In elementary school career awareness encompasses establishing the foundation of exposing kids to what is available in the world of work. The lessons and activities in this chapter will help you promote career awareness.

Indicators from ASCA National Model that are addressed in this chapter (see crosswalk pg 21):

A:A1.5 ....Identify Attitudes and behaviors which lead to successful learning

C.C2.3 ......Learn to work cooperatively with others as a team member

C:A2.8......Understand the importance of responsibility, dependability, punctuality, integrity and effort in the workplace

C:A1.3......Develop an awareness of personal abilities, skills, interests, and motivations

C:A1.2......Learn about the variety of traditional and non-traditional occupations

Chapter Contents

PRE-POST SURVEY FOR CAREER AWARENESS

Overview: To assess student perception on career awareness.

ASCA Indicator:
A:A1.5: Identify attitudes and behaviors which lead to successful learning.

Materials Needed:
Career Survey

Procedures:

1. Distribute Career Survey before the lesson(s) you intend to do on career awareness.
2. Compile the results to give you an idea of how the group/class feels about a career.
3. Repeat the survey at the end of the lesson(s) to assess what the students have improved on and how perceptions have changed.

Student Survey on Career Awareness

	Strongly Agree	Agree	Disagree	Strongly Disagree
I know what I want to be when I grow up.	❑	❑	❑	❑
I am aware of different careers at which I would be good.	❑	❑	❑	❑
I know the education required for the careers I am interested in.	❑	❑	❑	❑
I can identify the strengths I have that would help me in my career.	❑	❑	❑	❑

Striving for success without hard work is like trying to harvest where you haven't planted

— David Bly

Date:

Dear Parent/Guardian,

Every child has talked about what they might want to be when they grow up. They have dreamed about being a professional in a career that is in the far off future. Discussing future career opportunities is important even at the elementary level so that young people can have long-term goals, even if they change over time. For all intents and purposes, being a student is your child's current career. It is valuable for students to understand the importance of being a "professional student" and identify the link between the habits needed in the world of work to the habits students need to display at school. In our guidance lessons this week, we will be discussing career awareness. This would be a great time for you to talk to your child about what they might want to be when they grow up, why they have chosen that career, and what character traits they show at school that they would have to show in that job as well. Thank you for being part of your child's education, dreams, and goals.

Sincerely,

School Counselor

Activity 8.1

POETRY LINK

WHEN I GROW UP

Overview: This activity is a good introduction to discussing career exploration and thinking about what to do as a career in the future.

ASCA Indicators:
C:A1.3 Develop an awareness of personal abilities, skills, interests, and motivations

Materials: Poem pg 183

Procedures:

1. Divide the class into their office groups (see explanation on page 12).
2. Have the groups read the poem and prepare to present it in different ways. The groups can rap, sing, say it together, say one line per person, etc. Have each group practice and let one (or all groups perform).
3. Have students return to their desks and write a poem about what they might want to be when they grow up. Display *When I Grow Up* and the student's poem on a bulletin board.

Variations:

- For next lesson, have students apply for the job of poet (see job application in appendix). Select the best applicant and give the student a copy of the poem days before the lesson so they can practice how they would like to recite the poem. It is always nice to give them a tip/salary of a Payday® candy bar or a certificate of recognition for their effort.
- Assign each group a specific career. Have the groups create a poem about the career. Then the groups perform the poems for the rest of the class.

WHEN I GROW UP

BY TRACI KING

When I grow up, the question is, what would I like to be?
The answer's not so simple since so many choices I see.

Perhaps I'll be a doctor, and help people get well.
Perhaps I'll be a salesman with lots of stuff to sell.

A chef's not out of the question as I really like to eat.
And working with animals as a vet really would be neat.

As a cop it would be cool to help upkeep the law.
But if I was a carpenter I could use a power saw.

Maybe I'll aspire to be an anchor on the news.
Or a writer of a column, so I could express my views.

To be an actor might be fun but maybe I'm too shy
Or, perhaps a pilot after all — I really love to fly.

A teacher's real important to help kids think and grow.
Or maybe a famous dancer in a big hit Broadway show.

So many choices, so many careers, unique in their own way,
But do remember, I'm only 8 — don't have to know today.

Still, the one thing I will strive to be, even at this tender age,
Is to be the best me I can be and of course to get good grades.

Activity 8.2

STORY CONNECTION

CAREER DAY AT TYLER'S SCHOOL

Overview: This activity is a good introduction to discussing how school habits are similar to habits in the world of work.

ASCA Indicators:
A:A1.5: Identify Attitudes and behaviors which lead to successful learning

C:A1.3 Develop an awareness of personal abilities, skills, interests, and motivations

C:A2.8 Understand the importance of responsibility, dependability, punctuality, integrity and effort in the workplace

Materials: Story pg 185, Office Group Questions page 12.

Procedures:

1. Begin this lesson by asking students if anyone has thought about what career they will dress Career Day. Ask, "What do you remember from last year's career day?" Tell the students that you will read about a student who loves career day at his school.
2. Read the story aloud to the class. (If you'd like students to read silently while you read aloud, distribute copies)
3. After they have heard the story, divide the class into office groups (for explanation of office groups see page 12).
4. Assign one person in the group to be the question reader, and one person to be the secretary.
5. The Question Reader reads the questions to the office group.
6. The Secretary writes down the answer that the group discusses.
7. The group then discusses an optional story ending that they come up with for the last question. The Secretary will write the new story ending. (Option: these can be displayed on a bulletin board).
8. At the designated time, the class gets back together as a whole group and a group member can present one question that they discussed.

Activity 8.2

CAREER DAY AT TYLER'S SCHOOL

STORY CONNECTION

"Career Day is coming," said Mrs. Lavender. Tyler smiled and wiggled in his seat. He couldn't wait for Career Day. Tyler loved to dream of what he wanted to be when he grew up. He wanted to be a baseball player… or a doctor or a firefighter. Or a salesman or a pilot.

Each year on Career Day, he got to dream up new ideas of what to be when he got older. He loved the part of Career Day when he saw cars and trucks and anything on wheels and all of the jobs that went along with those wheels. And he loved to hear about different jobs from all different sorts of people.

So many things happened at his school on Career Day, he could hardly focus. This year, Tyler met someone who seemed to love Career Day as much as he did… his teacher, Mrs. Lavender. She called Tyler's class her 'professional students'. And Tyler believed her. He believed anything Mrs. Lavender said, because she seemed to know EVERYTHING! After all, how many teachers do you know that can name every

Mrs. Lavender was constantly reminding the class of their current careers as professional students. She reminded them of their professionalism any chance she got. She always said, "The habits of a career professional are much the same as a professional student."

When Jimmy was late for school, Mrs. Lavender whispered to him, "What if a pilot decided to come to work 2 hours late? The plane would leave for Boston without him… and they need him!"

When Nell didn't finish her work, Mrs. Lavender asked her, "What kind of reputation would a hair stylist have if she stopped the job halfway through?"

When Tyler and Skyler started arguing in line, Mrs. Lavender said, "Co-workers must get along. Even if you don't like who you work with, as a professional, you must be respectful."

When everyone in the class passed the math test. She gave them a "Payday Party."

When Karl admitted he forgot his homework, Mrs. Lavender told him that since he took responsibility in admitting his mistakes, he could postpone his deadline just this once.

And when Tyler's class met with their book buddies, Mrs. Lavender referred to the kindergartners as trainees.

Tyler loved being a professional student but it sure was hard work.

This year, when Career Day was approaching, Mrs. Lavender announced that one of the speakers was a student of Mrs. Lavender's from what she called "way back when."

When the day arrived, Tyler saw the man that used to be Mrs. Lavender's student named Mr. C. He was a lawyer who seemed to reach the sky. It was hard for Tyler to picture him sitting in a small desk learning math facts.

Career Day was just as great as Tyler had hoped. The next day Mrs. Lavender's class practiced being professional students by doing something Mrs. Lavender called "following up and showing gratitude." They wrote thank you notes to the speakers. Tyler chose the man who used to be Mrs. Lavender's student.

That night Tyler dreamt about coming back to Mrs. Lavender's class to talk about his career… or at least one of them!

Worksheet 8.2

Name: ____________________

Directions:
Answer these questions about the story you read.

1. What were some of the things about Career Day that Tyler liked?

____

____

____

2. What were some habits that Mrs. Lavender talked about that a professional student similar to a career professional?

____

____

____

3. How are the characteristics of a professional student similar to a career professional?

____

____

____

Optional ending.

—What do you think Tyler will be doing when he grows up?

—What do you think he remembers about what Mrs. Lavender taught him about being a professional student?

____

____

____

____

Activity 8.3

CAREER CENTERS

Overview: By setting up multi-sensory centers, students will have fun while learning about different careers using their different learning styles.

ASCA Indicator:
C:A1.2 Learn about the variety of traditional and non-traditional occupations

Materials: Bell or some noisemaker to indicate changing centers. See below for what is needed for specific centers.

Procedures:

1. Set up four areas in a classroom for four different activities that have career awareness content. Ideas for four centers are described below.

   Word Search Center
   Materials: Worksheet 8.3A, pencils

   Listening Center
   Materials: listening center with cassette player attached to headphones.

   Rappin' up Careers by Ken Smith and Arden Martinez

   Writing Center
   Materials: Worksheet 8.3B or 8.3C, pencils, crayons/markers

   Silent Reading Center
   Materials: books checked out from your school library (or in your personal library) that have career significance. Some good books include:

   Maze, S. *I Want To Be... Book Series,* Harcourt Brace (1997)

   Hopke, W. and Parramore, B. *Children's Dictionary of Occupational Titles*

   Krensky, S. *How Santa Got His Job*

   Krensky, S. *How Santa Lost His Job*

2. Divide students into office groups (see explanation page 12) and direct each office group to a specific center. Explain each center to the whole class verbally and if needed, have written directions posted by each of the four activities.

3. Have each group start at one center and have them participate in that center for approximately 6-7 minutes.

4. Ring a bell (or whatever noisemaker you have chosen to signify center change). When they are ready have them stand by their center. Have students point to their next center. (Direct them to go in a clockwise manner). Have them stand there pointing until you say "Now you may go to your next center."

Worksheet 8.3A

Name: ____________________________

ACTOR	CAREER
COUNSELOR	DOCTOR
FIREFIGHTER	LAWYER
MECHANIC	POLICEMAN
SCIENTIST	TEACHER
VETERINARIAN	WAITRESS

N M J M R L J B T P C P G C W
S A T L E S U F L V I Z W L C
C C I N Y R A U N U Q I U O W
E O U R W C U G Q S R M H D S
R S U Z A P O L I C E M A N A
E G T N L N F O W Z Q P R O T
T Y H D S L I A Y K U O Z S F
H H F S H E I R L R T T I M C
G D B V R T L O E C E T T E F
I K V T R B O O O T N E O C E
F T M E Z T G D R E E Z R H A
E H S M O J F J I K Y V O A M
R S A I R E H C A E T Q P N C
I T C Y D X S A C T O R I I D
F X U R M A J K G I R S S C Y

Worksheet 8.3B

CAREER GUIDANCE

Name: ______________________________

When I grow up, I might want to be a ______________________________

____

I would be good at this career because ______________________

____

____

____

____

Worksheet 8.3C

Name: ______________________________

Directions: Draw a picture of a career below and complete what you think the other requirements for this job should be.

To apply to be a _____________ you will need to be at least ______ years old.

You should be good at ____

____.

Please do not apply for this job if you are ______________________________

____.

This job pays _______________.We look to hire people who are __________

____

____

____.

Signed,
The Management

Activity 8.4

SHOW ME THE ANSWER CHARADES

Overview: Through this game, students will act out different careers.

ASCA Indicator:
C:A1.3 Develop an awareness of personal abilities, skills, interests, and motivations

C:A1.2 Learn about the variety of traditional and non-traditional occupations

Materials: Show me the Answer Charades, paper for each team to keep score (optional)

Procedures:

1. Divide students into groups or "office teams". Each team is assigned a career card.
2. Allow 5 minutes for teams to prepare their silent skits. They can do a silent skit together or one person in the group can be the actor.
3. All teams are given a small white board or piece of paper for each answer. The team writes down the answer of what they think each team is acting out but they do not show it until the facilitator says "SHOW ME THE ANSWER!"
4. Each team that answers correctly receives a point and the performing team receives the total correct points that their performance generated. (For instance, if team #1 did a charade of a hair stylist, and 3 out of the four groups answered correctly, they get 3 points and everyone who answered correctly gets one).
5. Each team will have 2 or 3 turns depending on time.
6. The group who has the most points is deemed the winner and they go to the final round.
7. In the final round, the winning team members will compete against each other in order to deem a career Charades Champion. Follow the same rules of scoring as above.
8. The winner receives a prize (attach a treat such as 100 Grand® Candy Bar to the certificate below.

Activity 8.4

CHARADE CARDS

POLICE OFFICER	PLUMBER
HAIR STYLIST	CHEF
TEACHER	CASHIER

Activity 8.4

CHARADE CARDS

WAITER/ WAITRESS	MAIL CARRIER
VETERINARIAN	PHOTOGRAPHER
SECRETARY/ ADMINISTRATIVE ASSISTANT	REAL ESTATE AGENT

Activity 8.5

LITERATURE LINK

HOW SANTA GOT HIS JOB

Overview: Using this literature link, students can take inventory about what is important to them in searching for a career.

ASCA Indicator:

C:A1.3 Develop an awareness of personal abilities, skills, interests, and motivations

C:A1.2 Learn about the variety of traditional and non-traditional occupations

Materials: *How Santa Got His Job* by Stephen Krensky

Procedures:

1. Introduce the lesson by talking to students about how important it is to find the right career that fits one's interests and abilities. It is important to consider certain qualities about oneself to determine which career might be a good fit. (For instance, someone who is scared of animals wouldn't be a good zookeeper or veterinarian.) Sometimes we have to try a few jobs to find out what you like and don't like about certain careers.

2. Today we're going to learn about how someone who tried many jobs before he found one that truly was a good fit. Let's read about how Santa got his job.

3. Read the book, pausing to do an "inventory" with the class on certain pages. There are many inventory questions that emerge from the story. For example:

   - On the page when Santa cleans chimneys stop and ask the students to raise their hands who wouldn't mind getting dirty on their job. Then ask who would not want to get dirty on the job.

   - On the page where Santa is delivering mail, ask if they would mind sitting in traffic in their job or to get to their job.

   - On the page when Santa works at a late night diner ask if they would want morning hours or a late night shift.

4. After the story discuss how Santa had to realize things about his abilities and personality that determined his job/ career. Depending on the students' age, you can ask them to think of people they know (relatives perhaps) and how their personalities make them better at their job.

Variations:

- Have the students do a "moving career inventory" by walking toward the side of the room designated for their likes or interests. (Working with people vs. things, outside job vs. inside job).

- A-Z Careers: Assign each student a letter. Then go through the alphabet and when their letter is called out they have to say a career that starts with that letter. If they can't think of one they say their letter and then" help please!"

Activity 8.6

CAREERS A-Z:

HOW MANY CAREERS CAN THERE BE?

Overview: Through this game, students will brainstorm many types of careers.

ASCA Indicator:

C:A1.3 Develop an awareness of personal abilities, skills, interests, and motivations

C:A1.2 Learn about the variety of traditional and non-traditional occupations

Materials: optional-magnetic letters or letters written on index cards, timer, paper for each team

Procedures:

1. Read poem *When I Grow Up* on page 183.
2. Introduce the topic for today's lesson is career awareness and today we will explore how many different types of careers you know. For instance you know the name of many careers such as: doctor, lawyer, teacher, professional athlete.
3. Ask students to close their eyes and think of as many careers as possible.
4. Explain that we will play a game to try to brainstorm even more types of careers.
5. Divide class into office groups (see page 12 for explanation) and distribute scratch paper to each team.
6. **Rules of the game:**
   - The counselor selects a random letter of the alphabet (either call out a random letter or pull a letter card or magnet out of a bag.).
   - Each team will have 30 seconds to brainstorm specific careers that start with that letter. Teams can write down their list of careers.
   - After 30 seconds, each team will have an opportunity to say one answer from their list. Teams will go one at a time and get a point if they can come up with a career that begins with the appropriate letter. Note that once a career has been called, the teams cannot use that specific career. For instance if the letter C is called, and the first team says Counselor, than no other team can say Counselor.
   - Depending on how many teams there are and the difficulty of the letter, do one or two rounds per letter. If a team has no answers they can say "pass" and get no points.
   - If the counselor is impressed with a unique and impressive career title there can be bonus points given. Additionally, depending on behavior, points can be added or subtracted.
7. After the game ask students if they heard any new career titles ?

Variations:

- Distribute Worksheet 8.6 and have students complete it.
- Provide large index cards or drawing paper to students with a letter of the alphabet on it. Have student illustrate a career of their choice that begins with that letter. Create a bulletin board display of "A-Z how many careers can there be?" with these drawings.

Worksheet 8.6

CAREERS A-Z:
HOW MANY CAREERS CAN THERE BE?

A ______________________________

B ______________________________

C ______________________________

D ______________________________

E ______________________________

F ______________________________

G ______________________________

H ______________________________

I ______________________________

J ______________________________

K ______________________________

L ______________________________

M ______________________________

N ______________________________

O ______________________________

P ______________________________

Q ______________________________

R ______________________________

S ______________________________

T ______________________________

U ______________________________

V ______________________________

W ______________________________

X ______________________________

Y ______________________________

Z ______________________________

Activity 8.7

EXPLORING CAREER GUIDANCE THROUGH RESEARCH

Overview: Students will research a variety of different careers to learn more about the skills required and the responsibilities involved in various careers.

ASCA Indicator:
C:A1.2 Learn about the variety of traditional and non-traditional occupations

Materials: *For this lesson you will need access to internet accessible computers and Worksheet 8.7B

Procedures:

1. Introduce this career technology lesson on careers by telling the class they will each have a job today since we are talking about jobs. The adults will be watching to see how you do with your specific responsibilities.
2. Summarize job roles. *Computer Specialists* will be typing into the computer and using the mouse, *Executive Directors* will be reading the directions and helping to oversee decisions, and *Administrative Assistants* will be writing down the answers that your group finds online and will present it to the class.
3. Divide the class into triads (groups of three). Within each group, assign each person one of roles: Computer Specialist , Executive Director, and Administrative Assistant. (You can pass out cards to each student with his /her job assignment on it (see cards below, and they can switch within their group if they choose to.)
4. Assign each group of three to one computer.
5. Distribute directions toworksheet 8.7A (page 202) to the *Executive Director* in each group and 8.7B (page 203) to the *Administrative Assistant.*

EXECUTIVE DIRECTOR

ADMINISTRATIVE ASSISTANT

COMPUTER SPECIALIST

Worksheet 8.7A

TECHNOLOGY CAREER GUIDANCE

Directions for Career Awareness Through Technology

1. First, the *Computer Specialist* should log on the computer and search for websites on careers. The Computer Specialist should handle the mouse for the group as decisions are made.

   Note: The group should have adult assistance when accessing the websites.

2. The *Executive Director* will decide on a career to research.

   a. The *Executive Director* should take a vote within their group to decide which specific job title the group will research.

   b. The *Executive Director* will tell the *Computer Specialist* which job title to research.

   c. The *Executive Director* will read the text on the web page aloud.

3. The *Administrative Assistant* should write down facts in each section, with the other group members helping to tell what to write down. The *Administrative Assistant* does the writing. If there is time the *Administrative Assistant* will present the interesting fact to the class.

**** REMINDER:***
You are coworkers and should do your best to work as a team.

Worksheet 8.7B

TECHNOLOGY CAREER GUIDANCE

Specific career that your group decided to research:

____

What responsibilities are involved in this career?

____

____

____

What is the salary or pay per hour for this career?

____

____

____

What is one other interesting fact you learned?

____

____

____

Activity 8.8

CAREER SCAVENGER HUNT

Overview: Students will be inspired to think about their career desires and the career choices of those around them in this fun interactive activity.

ASCA Indicator:
C:A1.3 Develop an awareness of personal abilities, skills, interests, and motivations

C:A1.2 Learn about the variety of traditional and non-traditional occupations

Materials: Worksheet 8.8

Procedures:

1. Ask students if they have a good sense about what careers there are in our society ?
2. Ask students if they know what careers their family members have? Ask if they want to do a career similar to a family member?
3. Tell students that in this game they will learn more about their friends and their friend's family.
4. Explain the rules of the game by reading the directions on the worksheet together: You will walk around the classroom and try to find people who can answer yes to the question in the box. They need to sign the space provided in the box. They will be asked to confirm their answers at the end of this activity. Who can get four in a row signed first?
5. Review the appropriate way to ask people the questions to get them to sign your paper.
6. Distribute the worksheet and remind students to put their name on their paper. Tell students that when the game is over I will count backwards from 10. By the time I get to one you need to be back in your seats.
7. Once one child has come up to you to tell you that they have four in a row, begin counting backwards from 10 as a cue for students to go back to their seats.
8. Verify the winning students answers by reviewing his/her answer sheet.

Worksheet 8.8

Name: ______________________

Directions: You will walk around the classroom and try to find people who can answer yes to the questions in the boxes. They need to sign their name in the space provided in the box. They will be asked to confirm their answers at the end of this activity. Who can get four in row signed first?

Do you want to go to college to prepare for a career?	Does someone in your family work at a doctor's office?	Do you want to be an animal trainer when you grow up?	Do you get to school on time everyday?	Can you think of three careers you might want to have when you grow up?
Does someone in your family work in a career that works with cars?	Do you want to be a professional athlete when you grow up?	Do you know anyone who has the career you would like when you grow up?	Does someone in your family work in a career that has night-time hours?	Do you want to make a lot of money when you grow up?
Can you think of two habits you need to have in school that you will also need in your career?	Do you think good behavior is important in a career?	Does someone in your family work in a career that they have to be polite to others?	Do you want to be a doctor when you grow up?	Do you know what kind of education you need for the career you want when you grow up?
Do you want to be a teacher when you grow up?	Does someone in your family work in a career that works with animals?	Do you always complete assignments on time?	Do you want to have a job in high school?	Does someone in your family travel often in their career?

Activity 8.9

JOB APPLICATION

Overview: Students will practice the skill of filling out a job application.

ASCA Indicator:
C:A2.8 Understand the importance of responsibility, dependability, punctuality, integrity and effort in the workplace

Materials: classified adds from the newspaper or an ad from an online career finding site, Worksheet 8.9, money certificate or homework pass

Procedures:

1. Introduce that the topic of today's lesson is how to explore careers that you might have in the future. Ask," What are some typical ways of finding a job?" (Show them the classified ads and discuss networking)
2. Go over the content of the job application. Define the term on references and discuss why it's important to make a good impression on those around you including teachers and bosses.
3. Tell students that they will fill out an application for their dream job.
4. Distribute Worksheet 8.9.
5. As students are working, the counselor should walk around and see who has good, appropriate answers.
6. When a majority of students are finished, ask students to put their pencils down and tell them that you are going to hire 2 people according to their applications. Give these students a salary of the Class Cash (see below).

Variation:

• Have students come to the front of the class for a mock interview using their application as questions to ask. Discuss the importance of being articulate and professional.

This "salary" entitles you ONE of the following:

A Free Homework Pass

Extra Computer Time

A Treat from your Counselor

Worksheet 8.9

JOB APPLICATION

What job are you applying for? ______________________________

Name ______________________ Phone Number ______________

Street Address ______________________________________

City, State, Zip ______________________________________

School ______________________ Grade __________________

Grades that you typically receive on your report card__________________

If we called your teacher, what things would she/he say about your work habits?

____

____

Why would you be good at this job? ______________________________

____

____

What would you expect the job responsibilities to be? ________________

____

____

References:

1. ____

2. ____

Thank you for your interest. Someone will contact you in the future if we would like to hire you.

Chapter 9

SETTING UP AN INNOVATIVE CAREER DAY

Career day is a fun way to infuse the career domain of a guidance curriculum into a school program. The week surrounding career day provide a great opportunity to teach career awareness lessons, and the entire week of a career day that can fill activities and games. In this chapter you will see how a successful career day can be organized. It is important to note that all schools will implement career day in different ways. This chapter might give you an idea for a framework or way to supplement a career day you have in place.

Indicators from ASCA National Model that are addressed in this chapter (see crosswalk pg 21):

A:A1.2 ....Display a positive interest in learning.

A:A1.5 ....Identify attitudes and behaviors which lead to successful learning

A:B2.6......Understand the relationship between classroom performance and success in school.

C.C2.3 ......Learn to work cooperatively with others as a team member

C:A2.8......Understand the importance of responsibility, dependability, punctuality, integrity and effort in the workplace

Chapter Contents

Activity ....*Page*

Chapter 9

GETTING STARTED:
HOW TO SET UP A CAREER DAY

Frequently Asked Questions (FAQs)

If I am the only counselor and have never done career day, how can I do it?

When you implement career day for the first time, start small. Choose one or two grade levels and have a career day for only those grades. This way you can become comfortable with the process and you can see what works and doesn't work for you. Also, by starting small you can build your base speaker contacts.

How many speakers do I need?

The number of speakers will depend on the size of your school. I would recommend no more than 30-35 students per class session. The formula I use for classroom speakers is as follows:

(Total # of students per grade level) divided by 30 = how many speakers in that grade level.

How should I recruit speakers?

There are a variety of ways to recruit speakers. Ask people with high interest jobs as well as charismatic speakers. I would recommend asking speakers rather than asking blindly if anyone wants to come.

For how long should I tell speakers to come?

Volunteer speakers should be there fifteen minutes before they expect to begin. For the younger students, speakers should speak for 15-20 minutes and the older students can have speakers for 20-30 minutes. I would not have students sitting listening to speakers for more than an hour and a half. They begin losing interest and the speakers begin to tire as well.

Do the speakers move around or do the students?

The speakers stay in one place so that they can set up their props, etc. The students rotate from class to class.

Striving for success without hard work is like trying to harvest where you haven't planted

— David Bly

Date:

Dear Parent/Guardian,

Career Day is on ____________. Career Day is a day when your child gets to hear about different opportunities in the world of work. Of course their career path won't start for quite some time, but elementary school is a time when children can be exposed to the different types of careers available and additionally they can see how their school habits are similar to the habits needed in the career world. This would be a great time for you to talk to your child about what they might want to be when they grow up. Thank you for being part of your child's education, dreams, and goals.

Sincerely,

School Counselor

SPEAKERS NEEDED FOR CAREER DAY

Date:

On ________________, our school will be having our annual Career Day. On this day, we need volunteers to speak to small groups of 2nd–5th graders. We would like the students to hear about different careers and understand the relevance of academic learning to the tasks they might someday perform in the working world. It is a great experience for the students of __________ to learn and explore the many different careers that exist in our community.

In preparing for this exciting day, we need to know if you would be willing to come in and talk about your career. We will send you more information in the weeks to come. Please return this form (or email me) to let me know if you are able to come. We appreciate all of your help in making our school a great place to learn.

Many thanks,

School Counselor
email____

phone ___________________________ fax ____________________________

Speaker's name ____

Career ____

Contact Phone # ____

Email Address ____

❑ I can be at career day on _________________ (date)
for the following time block(s):

❑ ________–________ am

❑ ________–________ pm

❑ Unfortunately, I'll be unable to be a career day speaker.

Please let us know by _______ if you will be able to make it!

Date:

Dear Career Day Volunteers,

Thank you very much for volunteering to speak at our ___________ Career Day on ___________ . You will be stationed in a classroom and present to students in the ___ grade. They will be rotating ___ different times listening to presentations of different careers. You will have approximately 15-20 minutes with each of the groups. Each group will have about 30 students and a teacher coming to hear your presentation.

Please check into the office by _____ and a student will show you where you will be presenting. You will have a student helper in your class at all times to help keep us all on schedule. The presentations will begin at _____ and conclude at _____.

Here are some ideas of things you can discuss in your presentation:

- The education/training required in your field.
- What a typical day in your career is like.
- What character traits are required in your career.
- Feel free to bring props, uniform, etc.
- Ask questions or play a game at the end and give away any career related trinkets to give to the students for answering questions about your career.

If you have any questions, please call us. If for some reason, a conflict arises and you cannot come for Career Day, please call us immediately so that we can plan a replacement speaker. We could not do this without the generosity of your time. Thank you on behalf of the students and staff at ___________ Elementary.

Sincerely,

School Counselor

Directions to our school: ____

____

____

CAREER DAY SPEAKER MAP

Directions: The speaker stays in one room and the class groupings rotate.

Schedule:

1st session .... 12:30 - 12:50pm
2nd session .... 12:52 - 1:12pm
3rd session .... 1:15 - 1:35pm

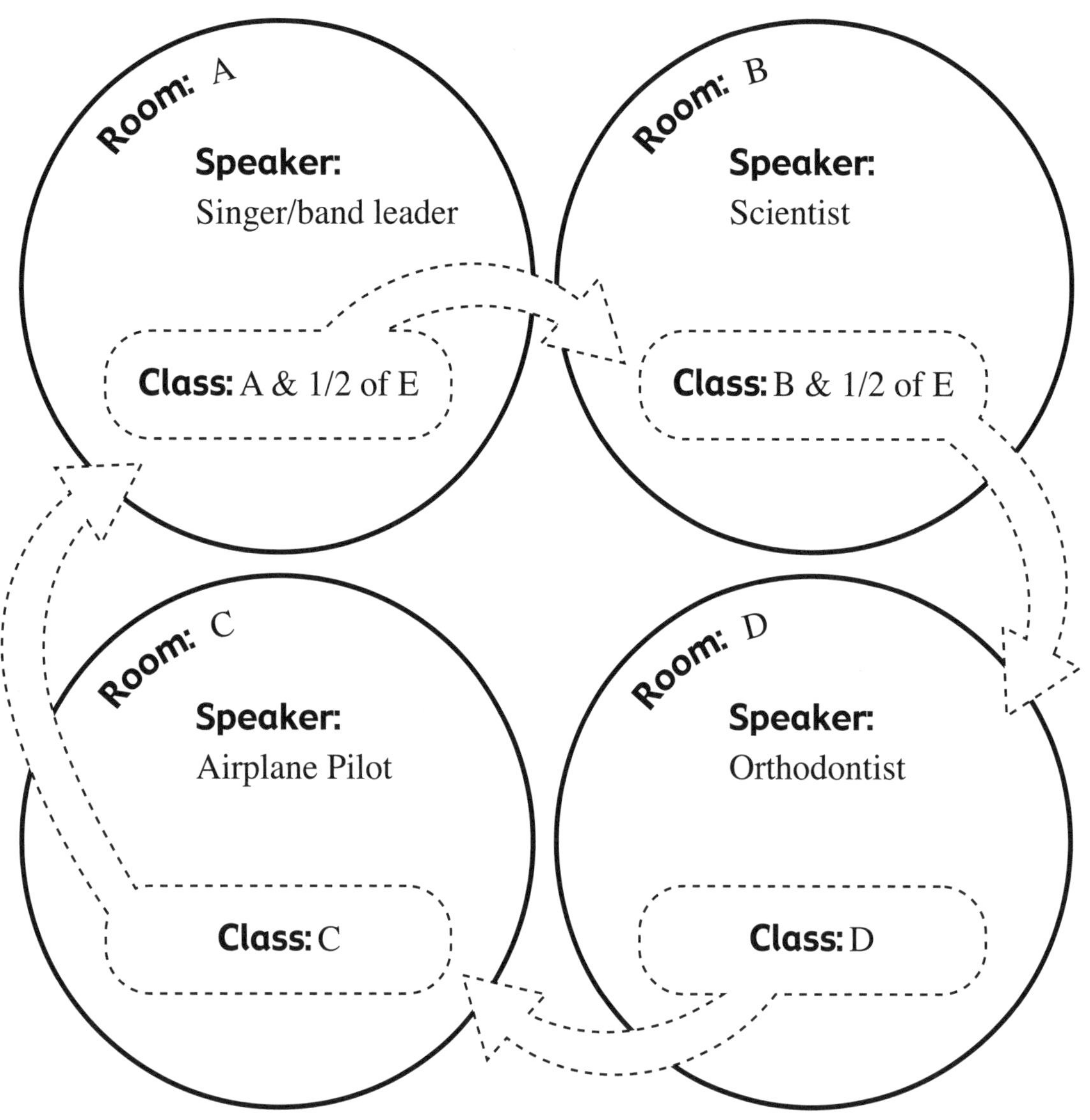

Teachers: You have a student helper who will let your speaker know when there are 2 minutes left. Then at the designated time for a session to finish, the helper will stand outside of the door until the other sessions are ready. Then rotate to your next session.

Thanks!
Your counselor

STUDENT NOTE TAKING

WHAT I LEARNED IN THE CAREER DAY SESSIONS

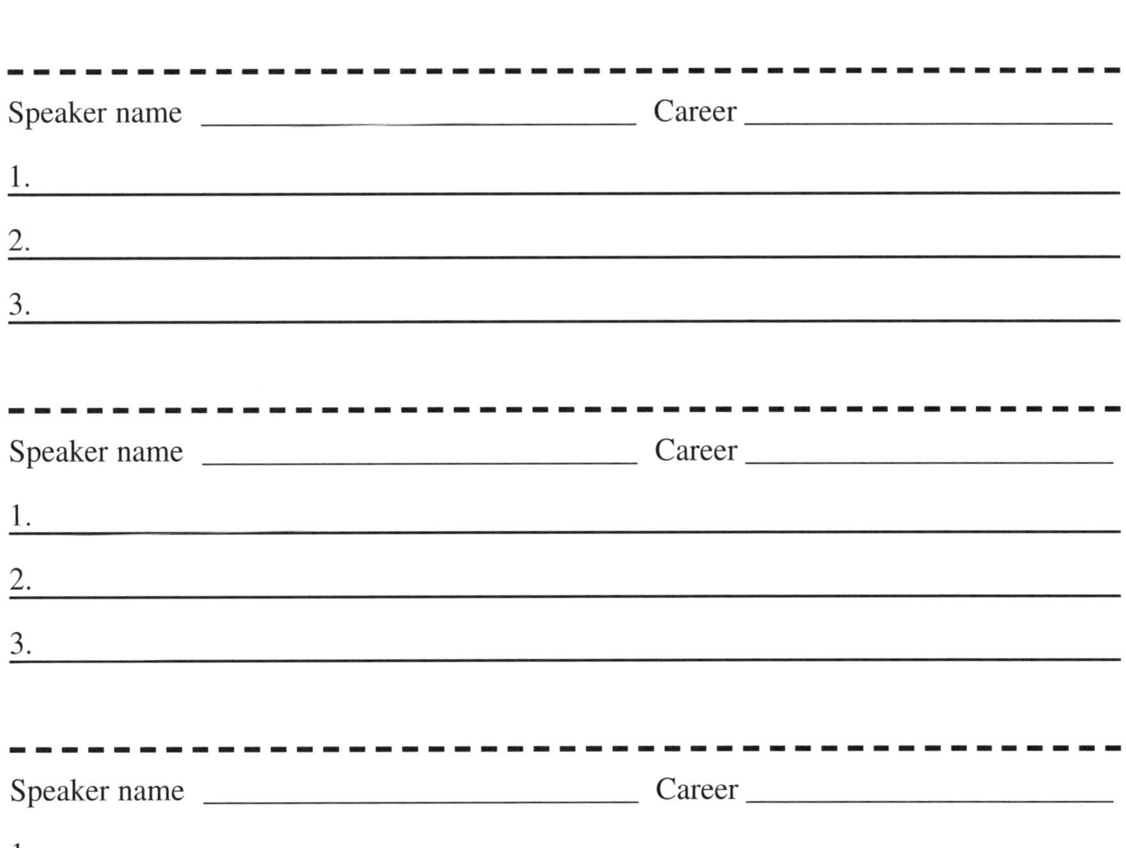

Speaker name ______________________ Career ______________________

1. ____

2. ____

3. ____

Speaker name ______________________ Career ______________________

1. ____

2. ____

3. ____

Speaker name ______________________ Career ______________________

1. ____

2. ____

3. ____

NAME CARD

-- (fold here) --

(write your name below and display it so that the speaker can see it)

CAREERS ON WHEELS

Careers on Wheels is an experiential way for students to learn about different careers. By inviting different cars, trucks, or anything that moves, students learn and enjoy the hands on learning. Each vehicle parks in front of a cone with a number on it and the classes rotate to 5 vehicles over an hour. (See map and schedule on page 214). Many times the students are allowed to sit in or see inside the vehicles.

THINGS YOU MIGHT NEED FOR CAREERS ON WHEELS

- Cones with numbers on them to designate stations where the vehicles will park.
- Bottled water to hand out to the speakers.
- Bull horn to let the group know when to change stations.
- Walkie-talkies to talk to the office to communicate about volunteers checking in.
- ____________________
- ____________________
- ____________________
- ____________________
- ____________________

Once you have implemented Careers on Wheels, use the space below to make notes as a reminder about how you want to tweak the process for the following year.

Date:

Dear Careers on Wheels Volunteer,

Thank you for volunteering to speak at our ________ Elementary Career Day for our Careers on Wheels program. You will be presenting to students who will be rotating to 5 different vehicle stations for 10-minute sessions. Each group will have approximately 20 students and a teacher coming to hear your presentation.

Please arrive by ___________. Someone will direct you where to park. The presentations will begin at _________ and conclude at _________. Since each rotation will last 10 minutes, you may decide to talk to the students for the first 7 minutes of the presentation and have students ask questions for the last 3 minutes. Some suggestions for topics that you may choose to cover in your presentation include:

- What a typical day in your career is like
- How your vehicle helps you in your job
- The education/training required in your field
- The character traits required in your job
- You can ask questions or play a game at the end and give away any career related trinkets to the students for answering questions

If you have any questions, please call us. If for some reason a conflict arises and you cannot come for Career Day, please call us immediately so that we can plan a replacement speaker. We could not do this without the generosity of your time. Thank you on behalf of the students and staff here at ___________ Elementary.

Sincerely,

School Counselor

Directions to our school: ____

____

____

CAREERS ON WHEELS CONTACTS

To prepare for Career On Wheels, create a master list of your local contacts.

Gas Light (utility truck) ______________________________

____

Limo ______________________________

____

Ambulance ______________________________

____

Fire Dept (fire truck) ______________________________

____

University Police (bicycle vehicles)______________________________

____

Police Dept. (motorcycle, truck, boat) ______________________________

____

Sanitation (sanitation truck) ______________________________

____

Post Office (Postal Truck)______________________________

____

SWAT team truck or Underwater Search and Recovery ______________________________

____

Plumber ______________________________

____

Cable or Telephone company ______________________________

____

National guard (hummer) ______________________________

____

TV or radio Station ______________________________

____

HERO unit (emergency vehicle through the Dept. of Transportation)______________________________

____

CAREERS ON WHEELS SCHEDULE

Career vehicles will be located_______ ___________. Please take your class outside and sit on the sidewalk in front of the assigned vehicle. A whistle blow will indicate when it is time to switch to your next vehicle.

During the time block where your class has a BREAK, please take your class inside for a bathroom and water break.

	9:15–9:25	9:27-9:37	9:39-9:49	9:51-10:01	10:03-10:13	10:15-10:25
1. Police Bicycles	Group A	Group B	Group C	Group D	Group E	Group F
2. Sanitation Truck	Group F	Group A	Group B	Group C	Group D	Group E
3. Police Robot	Group E	Group F	Group A	Group B	Group C	Group D
4. Post Office Truck	Group D	Group E	Group F	Group A	Group B	Group C
5. Cable Truck	Group C	Group D	Group E	Group F	Group A	Group B
BREAK	Group B	Group C	Group D	Group E	Group F	Group A

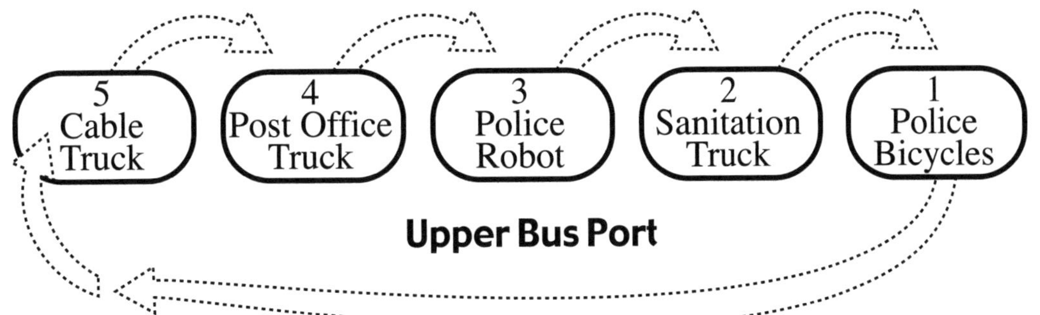

OVERVIEW OF CAREER DAY HELPERS

Career Day is typically a very busy day. There is much to do and lots of activity going on. There are many students who would be great helpers and assist in making career day more organized.

Who do you choose as a helper and how many helpers should you have?
It is important for career helpers to be responsible and have the ability to tell time to help keep the speakers on schedule. Depending on the size of your school and how many classes you have in each grade level will determine how many career helpers you have at each grade level. Typically having one career helper per volunteer speaker is effective.

How do you choose Career Helpers?
There are a couple of ways to select Career Helpers. You can use peer helpers if your school has a program, or you can have interested students apply to be a career helper by writing an essay on "How good habits at school are as important as good habits on a job." Have a panel of judges select the best essays to determine the career helpers. Also, you can simply have the teachers select one or two responsible students in their class to be a career helper.

SAMPLE LETTER FOR CAREER DAY HELPERS

Date:

Dear Parent/Guardian,

Congratulations! Your child has been selected by his/her teacher to be a Career Day Helper. Career Day Helpers are responsible students who will help the counselor(s) greet career day speakers and help to keep our speakers on schedule. We will have two training sessions so that your child knows just what to do on career day, which is on ____________. Career day helpers will participate in the day just like the rest of the students, but they will serve as leaders. We appreciate their help and congratulate them on being selected!

Sincerely,

School Counselor

- **Welcome and Congratulations!**

- **How to greet your Career Day Speaker**

  "Hello, and welcome to our school. Thank you for coming to Career Day. My name is _______________. Do you have any questions about the day?"

  Give them the provided bottle of water, a copy of their schedule and walk them to their classroom.

- **What do I need to wear?**

  Wear any appropriate and comfortable clothes. At this meeting we can decide if all career helpers should wear the same thing. Also, if you have a watch, please wear it on that day.

- **What are my responsibilities on that day?**

  You will come to the lobby to greet your speaker and walk them to their room.

  In the classrooms, you will serve as a "timer" for the speaker. When there are two minutes left in the session, you will have a sign that you will hold up to remind the speaker of the time limit.

- **When are you to come to the lobby to greet your speaker?**
  (write in appropriate time and date)

  ____

EXCUSE ME,

There are

two minutes

left in this session.

THANK YOU!

EXCUSE ME,

It is now

time

for us to go to

our next session.

THANK YOU!

GAMES AND ACTIVITIES
FOR THE DAYS SURROUNDING CAREER DAY

Staff Career Trivia Survey
Ask staff members to fill out the Career Trivia Survey (page 228). Each morning of the week surrounding career day, put a sign up in a prominent common place in the school (lobby, front door, etc.) which tells the facts of this person and have students guess who the facts are describing.

Guessing game: Who did this child grow up to be?
In this guessing game staff members are asked to bring in pictures from when they were in elementary school. These pictures are displayed in a prominent place in the school lobby or wall near cafeteria. See pages 229 and 230.

Promoting Writing Skills on Career Day
Provide your students a chance for students to read during the announcements. (See Page 231 for note to teachers)

Parent/Adult Interview
Encourage teachers to have their students interview an adult in their lives about their career.

Take home project
Teachers can send home a career day take home project with their students. In this project (page 233), students will create a paper doll of what they want to be when they grow up and put a picture of their face in the face of the doll. Classes can display their career paper dolls outside their classroom creating a school-wide atmosphere for career day.

Career Day Dress Up Contest or Parade
Make an announcement in newsletters and on the intercom that on Career Day, students may dress up as what they want to be when they grow up. Another way to add to this tradition is to have a parade. You can have judges standing along the parade who can give out Outstanding Career Dress Awards.

STAFF CAREER TRIVIA SURVEY

Please take the time to answer these questions. The students will enjoy learning more about you!

Name ______________________________

How many different careers have you had? ______________

What are some of your previous jobs?

____

____

____

When you were in elementary school, what did you want to be when you grew up?

____

____

____

What are some careers of your family members or relatives?

____

____

____

If you have any pictures of you in elementary school please put them in an envelope and put them in your counselor's box. I will scan them and get them back to you. The kids will love guessing "What did this person grow up to be?"

Please return this to your counselor by ______________.

GUESSING GAME:
WHO DID THIS CHILD GROW UP TO BE?

Staff members are asked to bring in pictures from when they were in elementary school. These pictures are displayed in a prominent place in the school lobby or a wall near the cafeteria. In this guessing game students can visualize that teachers were once kids like them who didn't know what they wanted to be when they grew up. This game is successful with students, teachers, and parents. Encourage teachers who bring in pictures to give hints as to which one is theirs. Have an envelope in the front office or outside your door for staff guesses and students guesses and give prizes to a winner in each group. Also, if you have one staff member who stumps everyone, you can reward him/her with a prize as well. Announce the real answers on the last day of the week surrounding Career Day.

Who Is She?

GUESSING GAME:
WHO DID THIS CHILD GROW UP TO BE?

These are all kids who grew up to choose a career here at our school.

Who could they be?

Turn in your guesses by ______________.

The answers will be posted that day
and the winners will be announced that afternoon.

(There will be a staff and a student winner... so don't share your answers!)

PROMOTING WRITING SKILLS

A CHANCE FOR STUDENTS TO READ DURING THE ANNOUNCEMENTS IN PREPARATION FOR CAREER DAY

Teachers,

For the week before Career Day (date ___________) we want to schedule morning readers on the intercom, telling us different components of career awareness. If you would like one of your students to read during that week, please contact me. You can reserve a slot for a student and tell me later which one it will be if you'd like to make this a classroom assignment/contest. Here are some ideas of what you can have students write (and read) about:

- Have students interview a family member about their career and write about it.
- Have students interview you about jobs you had before being an educator and have them write about it.
- Have students write about what they want to be when they grow up.

Let me know if you'd like to reserve a slot for a student to read during the announcements. We'd love to have your students read!!!

PARENT / ADULT INTERVIEW

Directions: Ask your parent or another adult the following questions. Then use this information to write a paragraph summarizing this person's career.

Q: What is your career?

A: ____________________

____

____

Q: How long have you been in this career?

A: ____________________

____

____

Q: What do you like best about your career?

A: ____________________

____

____

Q: What character traits are necessary for your career?

A: ____________________

____

____

Q: Before this job, what were some other jobs you have had?

A: ____________________

____

____

Q: What things did you learn in school, that helps you in your career?

A: ____________________

____

____

Paragraph Summarizing the interview:

____

____

____

____

____

____

____

____

TAKE HOME PROJECT
FOR CAREER WEEK

Directions: Take this home and place a picture of you in the circle on the head of the figure. Then, decorate the body with a uniform or outfit of what you might be when you grow up. These will be displayed in the hallway during Career Week.

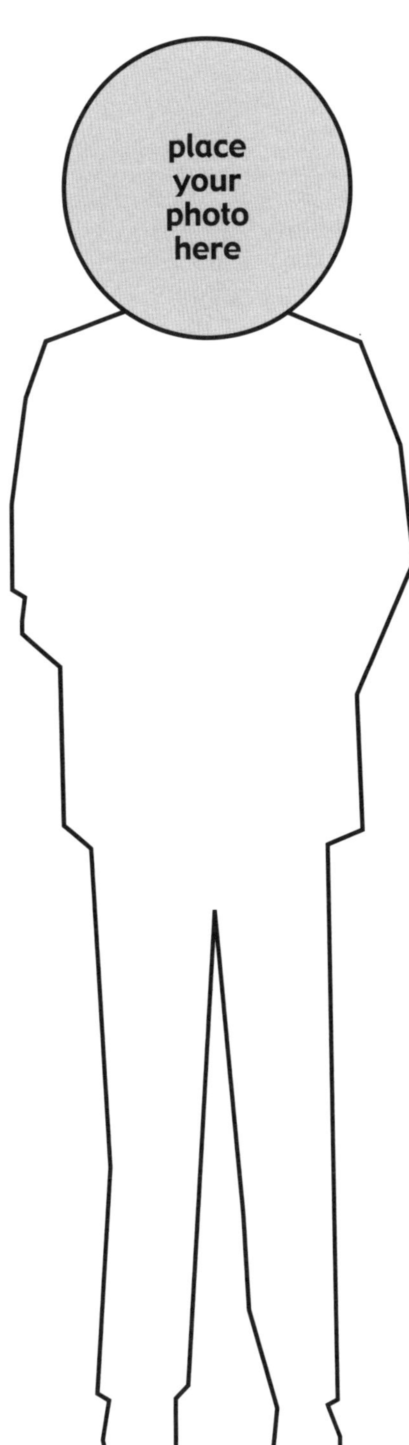

TEACHER CAREER DAY NEEDS ASSESSMENT

Grade level __________

Thank you for your support and your help as always!

Your counselor

1. Do you think the length of time per speaker was appropriate? Too long? Too short?

____

____

____

2. For next year, how many speakers do you think would be ideal for your grade level?

____

____

____

3. Did the transitions go smoothly? What would you do differently?

____

____

____

4. Next year we plan on continuing to recruit high interest speakers. Do you have any ideas of what types of careers your students would be interested in?

____

____

____

5. Do you have any other feedback for us regarding Career Day?

____

____

____

____

____

____

Thank you for your support in this school-wide program!

APPENDIX A

Appendix A

MAKING THE LINK GAME

Overview: This game integrates the nine school success skills that are taught in this program.

ASCA Indicators:
A:A1 Improve Academic Self-Concept

A:A2 Acquire Skills for Improving Learning

A:A3 Achieve School Success

C:A1 Develop Career Awareness

C:C2 Apply Skills to Achieve Career Goals

Materials: Make a Link Score Cards (for as many teams you have) page A.1, Game Board (pages A.2-A.3) *[reproduce this game board on 11x17 paper and laminate onto a card stock or construction paper background]*, Link Question Cards for each subject covered in the book (pages A4.-A?), game pieces, and dice

Procedure:

1. Explain to class that this game will review the skills we have learned in the past few lessons and we will review skills that will help you be better professional students.

2. Divide the class into two teams: ***The Professionals*** and the ***Study Smarts*** (or you can let them make up their own names). Each team has a Make a Link Score card (reproduce page A1). The score cards can be set on a desk in front of each team

3. Explain that one person from each team will come up to the game board (pages A2-3). The first player will roll the die and move that many spaces. If they land on a space with an icon, they have to choose a card from the correlating category of question cards (page A4-A?). If they answer correctly, they get to place the card on their scorecard in the designated place for that category. The object of the game is to try and earn a card from each category. So, if my team has already earned a card from the time management chapter, next time they want to land on a space with a different icon.

4. The player from the other team then has a turn. After both of these contestants have had their turn, two more teammates come up and represent their team.

5. **Note:** There are cards within each category that are called "Wild Links". If a student can tell us one thing a professional student should do to succeed, then they get to put the wild link on any category spot on the Score Card.

6. Remind students that they are professionals, and need to be respectful. The counselor has extra Wild Link Cards as incentives for the professional team as their "raise" for doing a good job. While no one is going to get "fired", in this game professional students can have one of their category cards taken away if they are noisy or disrespectful.

7. At the end of the time limit, the team with the most category spaces filled on their scorecard is deemed the winner.

** Note that even if you don't cover all chapters' categories, this game is easy to play to reinforce academic skills.*

Appendix A.1

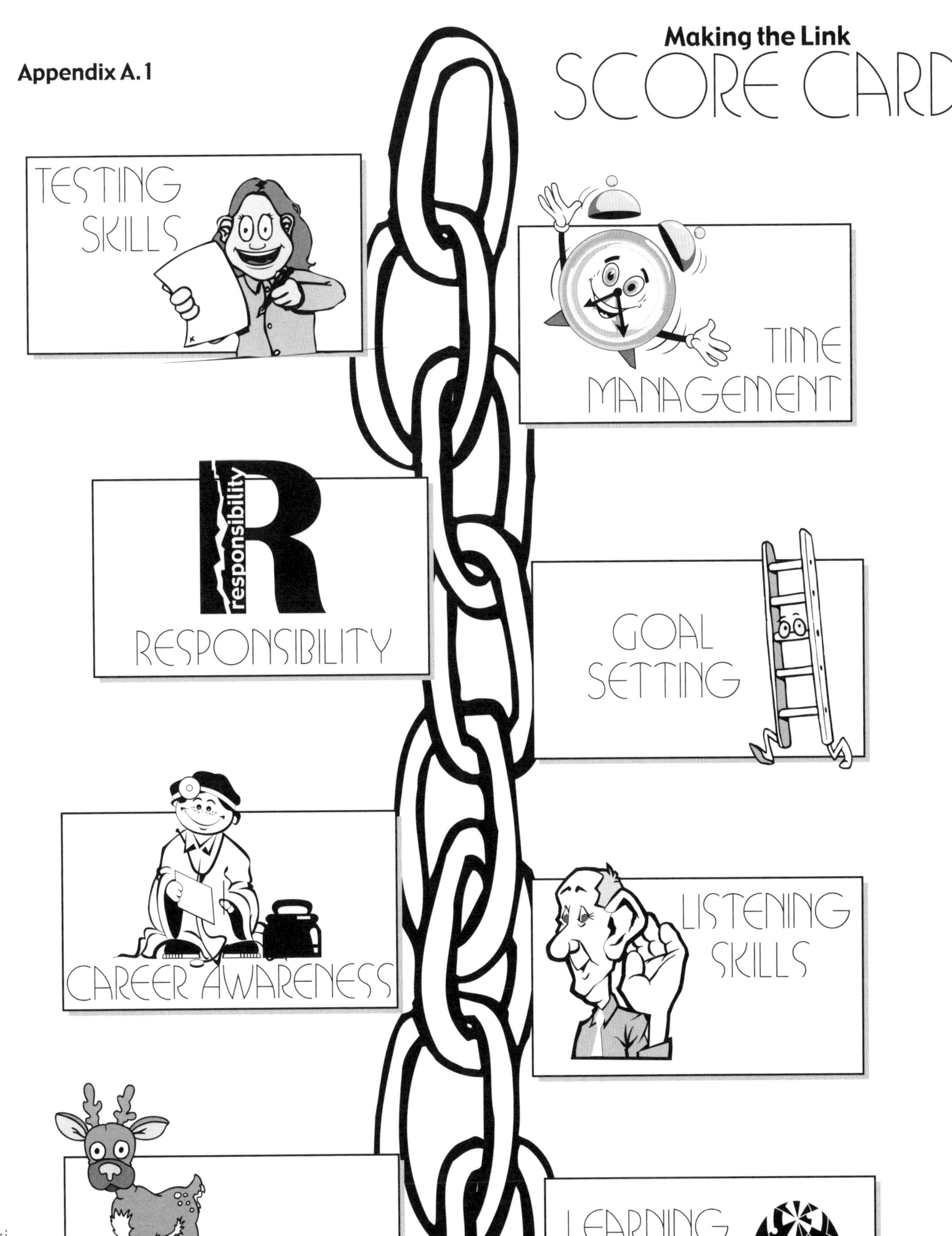
Making the Link
SCORE CARD
TESTING SKILLS
TIME MANAGEMENT
responsibility
R
RESPONSIBILITY
GOAL SETTING
CAREER AWARENESS
LISTENING SKILLS
LEARNING FROM MISTAKES
LEARNING STYLE

Making the Link

GAME BOARD

Making the Link
GAME BOARD
responsibility
R
responsibility
R

MAKING THE LINK GAME
QUESTION CARDS

Time Management

These are the "Time Management" question cards for the Making the Link Game (see directions on page 236).

Tell about a time you were late for school. How did you feel?

Do you think other students notice when you are late for school? Why?

Say this sentence out loud:

"Time management is very important."

Name someone in your class who has never been late for school.

How do adults feel when they are late for an appointment. Why?

Tell about a time an adult was late taking you somewhere.

Say this sentence out loud:

"Being on time is respectful to those who are counting on you."

What is a consequence for you if you are late to school?

What does punctuality mean?

Tell us what time it is right now.

WILD LINK CARD
If you tell us one skill that helps you be a professional student, you can put this card on any category space on your scorecard.

WILD LINK CARD
If you tell us one skill that helps you be a professional student, you can put this card on any category space on your scorecard.

Appendix A.3 — BACK

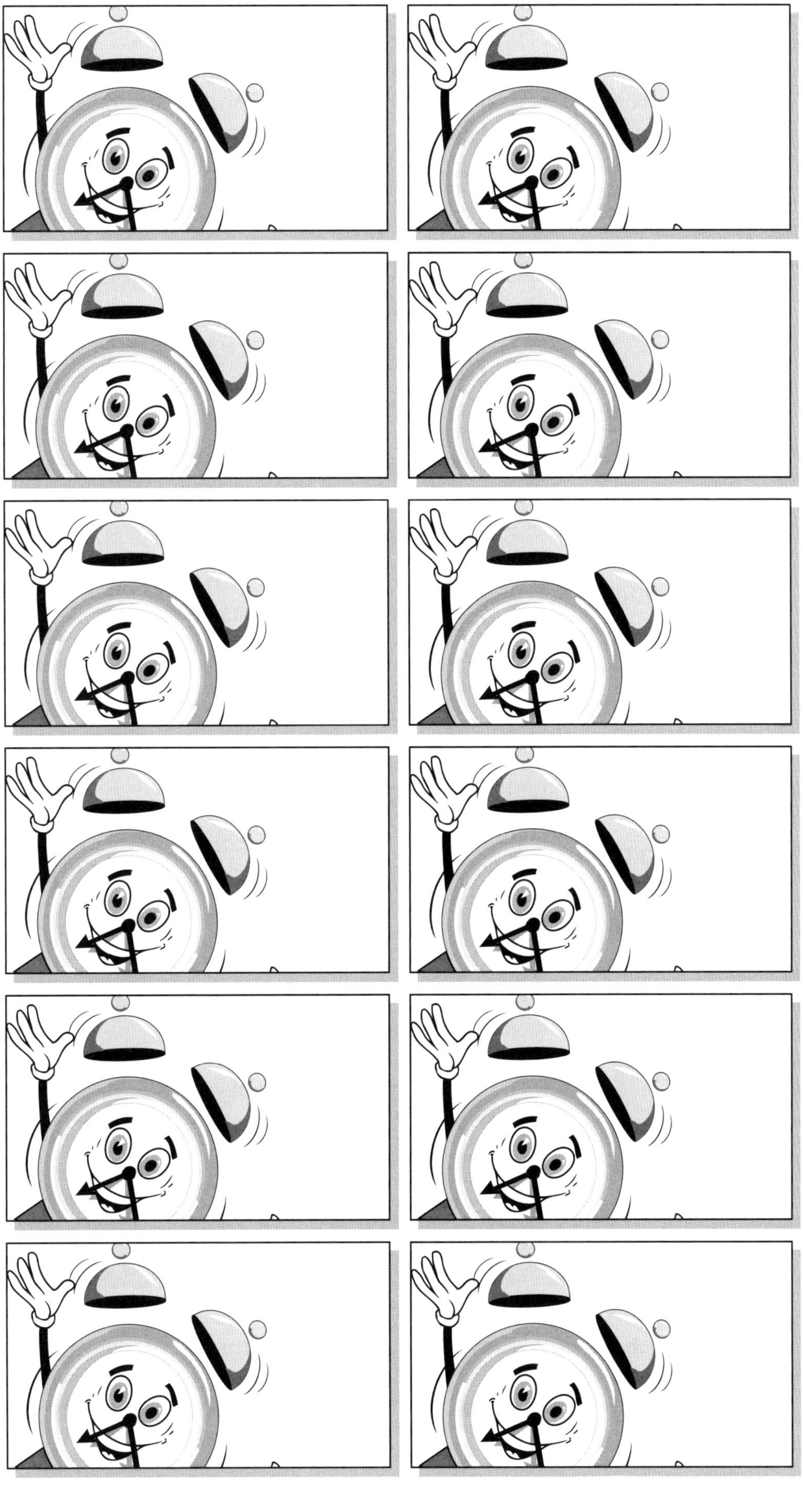

Responsibility

These are the "Responsibility" question cards for the Making the Link Game (see directions on page 236).

Tell about a time you were not responsible about finishing your homework. How did you feel?

Do you think other students notice when you are irresponsible? If you are responsible do they notice?

Say this sentence out loud:

It is very important to be responsible.

Name someone in your class who is very responsible. How does he/she show responsibility?

How do adults feel when they are irresponsible?

What is an important responsibility for a teacher at work?

Say this sentence out loud:

Being on time is respectful to those who are counting on you.

What is a consequence for you if you are responsible?

What does responsibility mean?

Tell us what responsibilities do you have at home?

WILD LINK CARD
If you tell us one skill that helps you be a professional student, you can put this card on any category space on your scorecard.

WILD LINK CARD
If you tell us one skill that helps you be a professional student, you can put this card on any category space on your scorecard.

Appendix A.4 — BACK

responsibility R	responsibility R
responsibility R	responsibility R
responsibility R	responsibility R
responsibility R	responsibility R
responsibility R	responsibility R
responsibility R	responsibility R

Goal Setting

These are the "Goal Setting" question cards for the Making the Link Game (see directions on page 236).

Tell about a time you set goals to complete a group project.

Tell about short-term goals.

Say this sentence out loud:

It is very important to set goals.

Tell about long-term goals.

How is setting goals like climbing a ladder or a mountain?

What are some things that get in the way of accomplishing goals?

Say this out loud:

In order to accomplish a goal, you must make small steps along the way.

Do you challenge yourself when you set goals?

What is an example of a goal a professional baseball player might have?

Why is goal setting important to businessmen/women?

WILD LINK CARD

If you tell us one skill that helps you be a professional student, you can put this card on any category space on your scorecard.

WILD LINK CARD

If you tell us one skill that helps you be a professional student, you can put this card on any category space on your scorecard.

Appendix A.5 – BACK

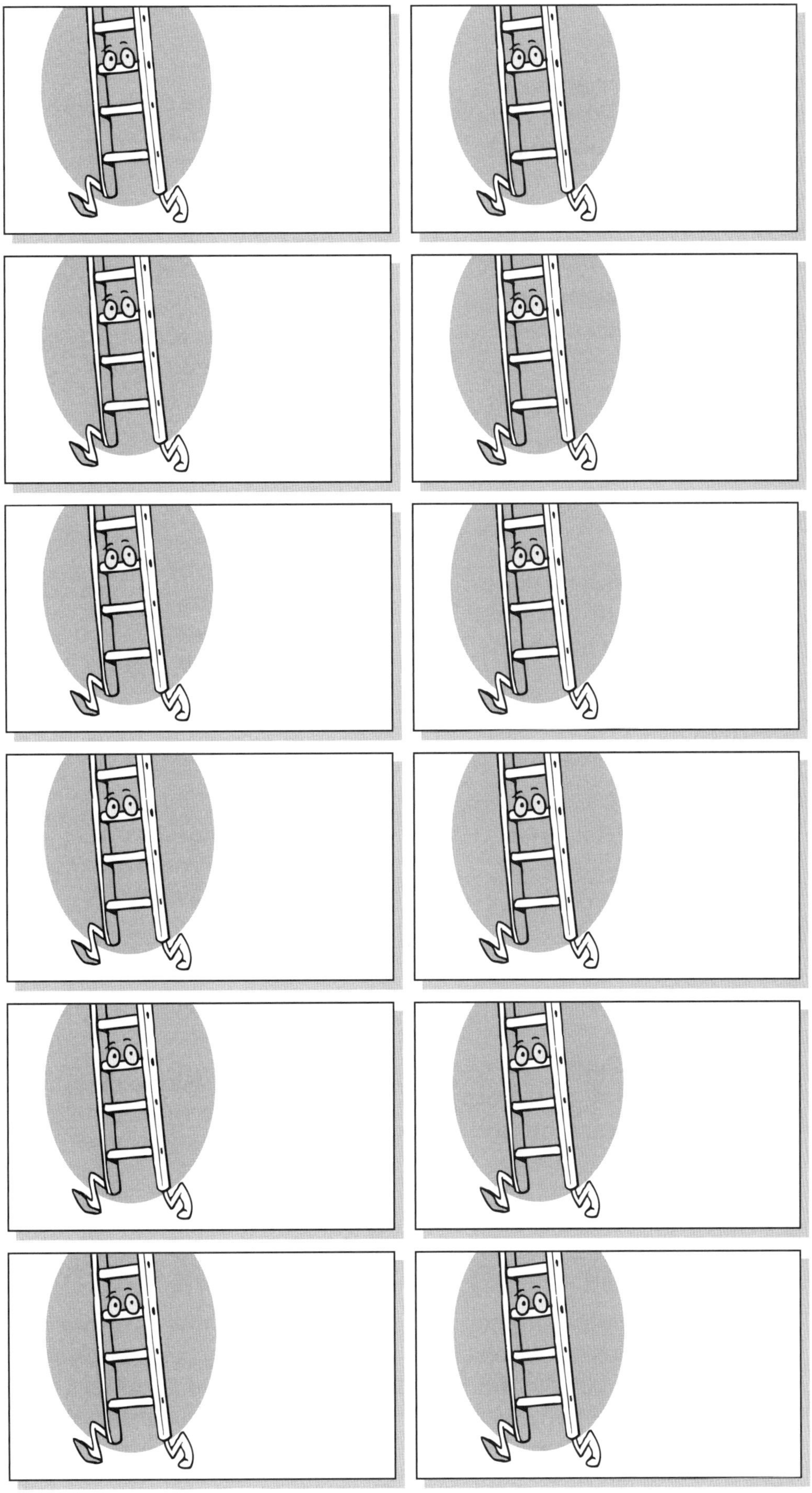

MAKING THE LINK GAME
QUESTION CARDS

Learning From Mistakes

These are the "Learning From Mistakes" question cards for the Making the Link Game (see directions on page 236).

What are some common mistakes that kids your age make?

How do people cope when they make mistakes?

Say this sentence out loud three times:

Everyone makes mistakes.

Name two feelings that you have when you make mistakes.

Name a small mistake you have made this week. How did you handle it?

Have you ever made a mistake on doing homework? How did you feel?

How can you avoid making mistakes in class work?

What do adults do when they make mistakes in their careers?

Do teachers ever make mistakes? What does your teacher do when he/she makes mistakes?

What is a mistake that someone in your family has made?

WILD LINK CARD
If you tell us one skill that helps you be a professional student, you can put this card on any category space on your scorecard.

WILD LINK CARD
If you tell us one skill that helps you be a professional student, you can put this card on any category space on your scorecard.

Test Taking Skills

These are the "Test Taking" question cards for the Making the Link Game (see directions on page 236).

Tell about a time you forgot to study for a test.	Do you think other students notice when you are nervous on a test?
Say this sentence out loud three times: **It is very important to be prepared for a test.**	Describe a person who is responsible about studying for tests.
Name three adults who would be proud of you if you get a good grade on a test	What is an important things to do the night before a test?
What are some healthy foods to eat on the morning before a big test?	How do you prepare for tests?
Name three feelings you have about taking tests.	Tell us about a test you did well on.
WILD LINK CARD If you tell us one skill that helps you be a professional student, you can put this card on any category space on your scorecard.	**WILD LINK CARD** If you tell us one skill that helps you be a professional student, you can put this card on any category space on your scorecard.

Appendix A.7 — BACK

MAKING THE LINK GAME
QUESTION CARDS

What are some ways that a visual learner should study?

Why is it important to know your learning style?

Say this sentence out loud three times:

Everyone learns differently.

What are the three learning styles?

Learning Styles

These are the "Learning Styles" question cards for the Making the Link Game (see directions on page 236).

What learning style is the easiest for you?

What does kinesthetic mean?

What styles of learning do your friends in your class use?

How often do adults learn new things in their careers?

Learning the ABC song is learned from auditory learning. Sing the ABC's.

When you learn something by seeing it on TV, what type of learning style is that?

WILD LINK CARD
If you tell us one skill that helps you be a professional student, you can put this card on any category space on your scorecard.

WILD LINK CARD
If you tell us one skill that helps you be a professional student, you can put this card on any category space on your scorecard.

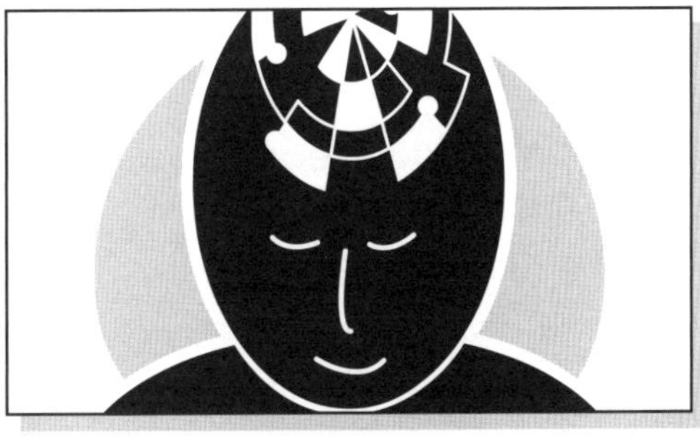

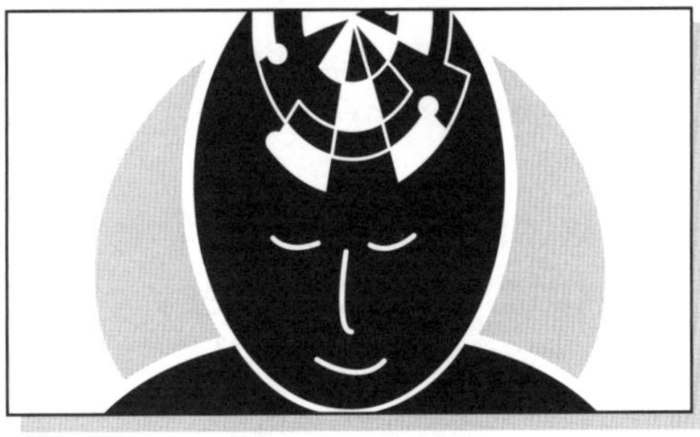

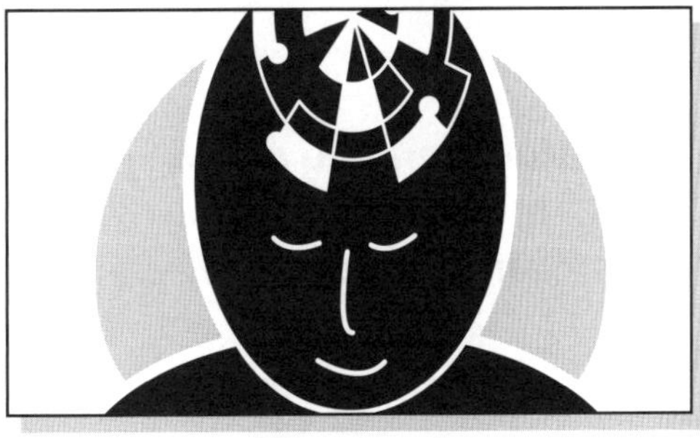

MAKING THE LINK GAME
QUESTION CARDS

Listening Skills

These are the "Listening Skills" question cards for the Making the Link Game (see directions on page 236).

What are reasons it is important to listen in school.

Name three ways for people to know you are listening.

Say this sentence out loud three times:

Listening and paying attention are very important skills.

Name two feelings that you have when someone doesn't listen to you.

Tell about a time when you didn't pay attention to what your parents said because you were watching TV

Who is a good listener in your life?

How can you avoid making mistakes in class work?

Why is it important for adults to listen or pay attention in their careers?

Do teachers ever have a hard time listening? Why?

What are some things that distract you from paying attention in class?

WILD LINK CARD
If you tell us one skill that helps you be a professional student, you can put this card on any category space on your scorecard.

WILD LINK CARD
If you tell us one skill that helps you be a professional student, you can put this card on any category space on your scorecard.

Appendix A.9 — BACK

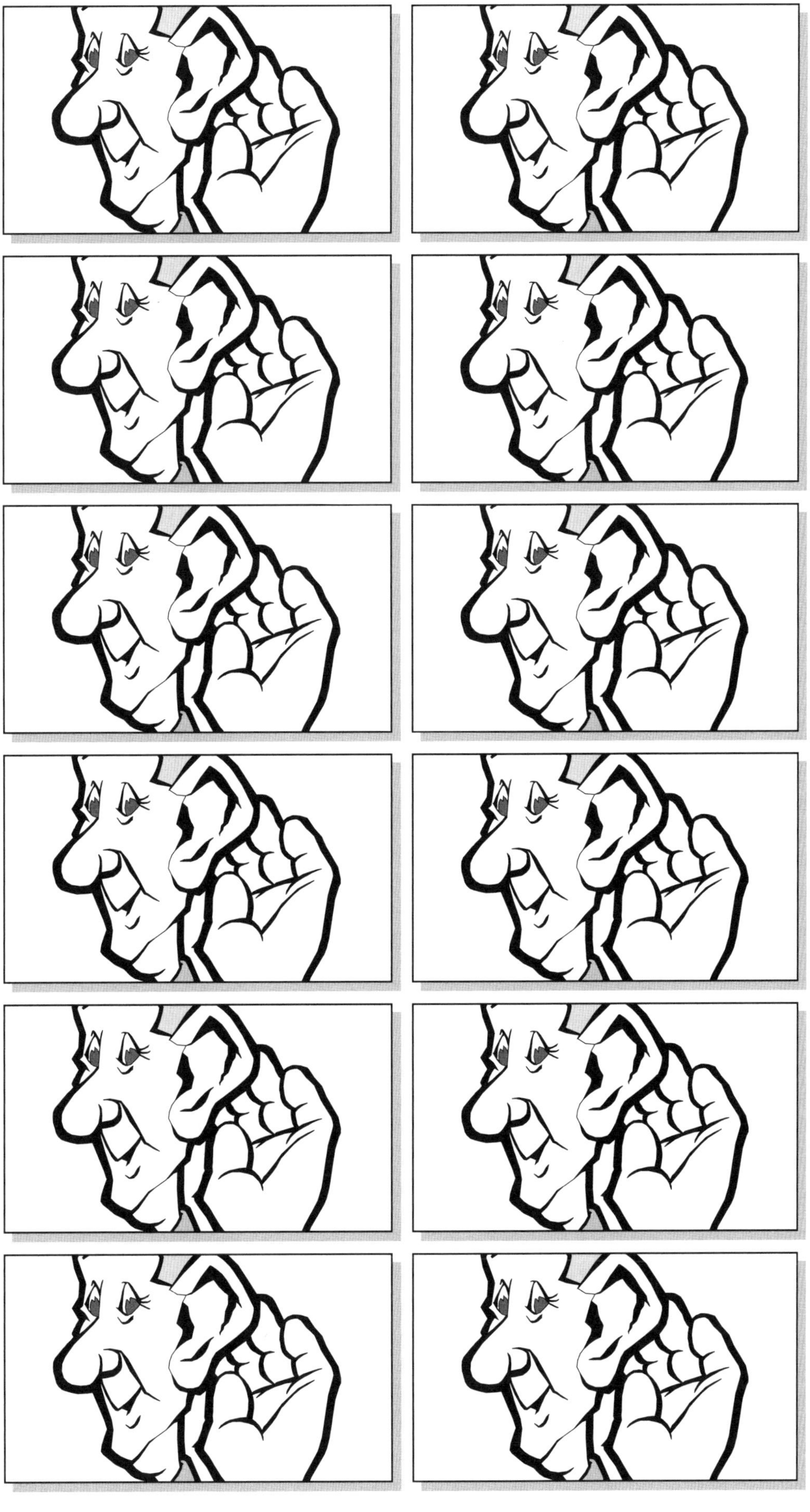

MAKING THE LINK GAME
QUESTION CARDS

Career Awareness

These are the "Career Awareness" question cards for the Making the Link Game (see directions on page 236).

What do you want to be when you grow up?

How do adults show responsibility in theirs careers?

A doctor must get along with many people in the career. Who must a doctor get along with?

How is education important in getting a job?

What happens to people who show up late to work?

Why is behavior important at school? Why is behavior important in a career?

Name the careers that people have in your family.

What subjects are you good at? What careers would you be good at using those skills.

How do people get a job?

Pick a letter of the alphabet. Name three careers that start with that letter.

WILD LINK CARD
If you tell us one skill that helps you be a professional student, you can put this card on any category space on your scorecard.

WILD LINK CARD
If you tell us one skill that helps you be a professional student, you can put this card on any category space on your scorecard.

REFERENCES

American School Counselor Association. (2003). *The ASCA national model: A framework for school counseling programs*. Alexandria, VA: Author.

Bowers, J.L. and Hatch P.A. (2002). *The National Model for School Counseling Programs.* Alexandria, VA: American School Counselor Association

Jones, C F. (1991). *Mistakes That Work.* New York: Doubleday.

Finchler, J. (2000). *Testing Miss Malarkey.* Walker & Co.

Krensky, S. (1998) *How Santa Got His Job* New York: Simon & Schuster Books for Young Reader

Shapiro, L. E. (1994) *The Very Angry Day That Amy Didn't Have.* Pennsylvania: The Center for Applied Psychology.

Shannon, D. (2002) *David Gets in Trouble.* New York : Blue Sky Press.

Stanley, D. (1992) *Moe the Dog in Tropical Paradise,* New York: Putnam.